MAINE
Unleashed

101 Off-Leash Walks in Maine

Mid-Coast Edition

By Dr. Linn Caroleo, Daisy M. & Yogi B.

Produced by
LONE WOLF Enterprises, Ltd.
www.lonewolfent.net

Maine Unleashed: 101 Off-Leash Walks in Maine

ISBN 978-0-9821102-0-1

Printed and Bound by: Lightning Source Inc.

Sponsoring Editor: R. Dodge Woodson

Production Supervisor: Virginia Howe

Copy Editor: Wendy Lochner

Proofreader: Leona Woodson

Art Director: Virginia Howe

Composition: Lone Wolf Enterprises, Ltd.

Publishing Consultant: Creative Consulting, Inc.

Front cover photo: By Linn Caroleo. Daisy and Yogi walking from Bliss Woods to Sayles Field, Freeport, Maine—2008.

Back cover photo: By R. Dodge Woodson

*This book is dedicated to all the dogs out there
and their adventure seeking owners.*

To Lucy, we miss you.

Acknowledgments

This is my first book, and it has been a labor of love, joy, frustration, and invigoration. Maine is a beautiful state, one that affords both residents and visitors with beautiful natural settings, spectacular coastlines, hills, vistas, open spaces, wildlife, and more. I hope this book guides you to a special place that you revisit often with your loved ones.

Due to problems arising from knee surgery I trained my dogs Daisy and Yogi to obey off-leash commands. With a combination of patience, praise, and treats, the dogs now respond to the silent 12-second-rule (return to Linn if out of sight for 12 seconds). They are my loyal companions. They always have fun on the trail. They never complain. And they have helped me find our way back to the truck more than once when I had turned off the marked trail thinking I knew where we were (and had left the compass in the glove compartment).

Walking with your dog is fun and good exercise, but many places are only leash- or people-friendly. This book is unique in that I tell you where to go if you, like me, prefer your dogs to be free to explore, run, and romp on their own. Tests have shown that dogs who problem-solve and have the freedom to run regularly off-leash are better adjusted and smarter than their leashed backyard relatives.

Many people and dogs helped me put this book together. Without word of mouth, talking to locals, and asking for directions I would never have found even half of these places. New to Maine, I was determined to see as much as possible in a short period of time. I want to thank all of those who helped me, took the time to talk to me, and joyously encouraged me to complete this book.

Please enjoy these walks. Some are short, some are long, some are loops, some have places for your dogs to go swimming, and most are accessible year-round. All the trails are enjoyable and are great outdoor trekking excursions.

A special thanks to Daisy and Yogi, who tirelessly went with me more than once to all these and many other locations. My husband, your undying support and willingness to let me take the time to complete this book is a wonderful dream come true for me. Thank you, Kate; your expertise was the backbone I needed to stay on task. Cody, Mattie, Mary, Bella, Rebecca—you were my first guinea pigs and my very enthusiastic cheering section. Dave, Beverly, Basha, Minnie, Saga—you never let me down and always showed eager interest in everything I came up with. Melissa, thank you—you are the best dog-sitter in the world. May the entire Wolf Pack, both big and small, never stop howling at the moon.

To contact me with comments, write to linn@aikorn.com.

PHOTO: WAYNE CAROLEO

Thank you, Linn :-)

Preface

by Kate Farnham
  Registered Maine Guide

Miles and miles of trails wind through mid-coast Maine.
Linn Caroleo has revealed 101 "off the beaten path"
refuges to walk your four-legged friends. This book is for
those people who are nourished by the outdoors and
love to share that freedom to roam with their dogs. *Maine
Unleashed* is a compilation of romps for dogs and their
owners that gives the opportunity for off-lead gallops in
solitary forested settings that are the antithesis of dog
parks. This book tempts the urban dog walker to step off
the sidewalk and into nature. To those who vacation in
Maine with their pet, it gives opportunities far beyond a
restricted walk around the hotel parking lot. Throw Fido
in the car, grab a picnic lunch, and head for one of several
coastal gems that meander through salt marshes or vistas
to the ocean. Both loyal friend and master or mistress will
be pleasantly surprised by the beauty and scenery that
Caroleo creatively narrates in her entries.

Each of the 101 entries is unique. They are places that are
frequented by the dog savvy folks who realize the impor-
tance of allowing their dogs the "under voice command"
freedom to fulfill their curiosities, snouts to the ground
and tails wagging in the air.

Paws down, this book has been voted number one by the
vast majority of fuzzy companions. Walking your dog
off-lead on these safe and dog-friendly jaunts has a great
number of healthy benefits for you and Fido, accolades
that include a more active pet, doggie socialization, and a
natural setting to hone behavior. Caroleo leads us on dog
walks through enchanted forest loops that culminate in
gushing waterfalls and mossy covered rocks around which
gurgling brooks flow. There are no bones about it—these
places will be revered by any dog who loves to settle into a
pool of cool water and come out shaking!

Introduction

Daisy is a four-year old, black, American Field style Labrador Retriever. She has severe hip dysplasia and arthritis in her forearms. She dictates the difficulty of the trails that have been included in this book, since she is unable to climb excessively steep inclines. She loves water, but only wades and lies in shallow water; she seldom swims. She favors trails that are soft green moss or pine needle covered. She loves to chase deer, and has been known to get us off track by following their scent. Her favorite place is Fort Popham Beach.

Yogi is a two-year old silver Labrador Retriever. He is often mistaken for a Weimaraner, but if you look at him closely you can see he is a true lab (AKC chocolate). He loves water and sticks. He prefers to swim and will jump off rocks into the deep water after a stick. He is a very healthy boy and often leads us off the beaten path chasing a wild turkey. He favors trails that include freshwater swimming and perhaps a bird or two. He has met skunks and porcupines and I've encouraged him to stay away from those characters. His favorite walk is Center Pond.

Dr. Linn Caroleo lives in Maine with her husband and these two dogs. She teaches mathematics at Southern New Hampshire University during the school year. She takes pictures on a regular basis, but she does not consider herself a professional. She is originally from Norway, but has lived in the United States for over 20 years. This is her first book, and she hopes to write similar books for other New England states.

Part of the proceeds from the sale of this book will be donated to the various conservation groups who do the maintenance on these wonderful trails.

Walk Scoring and Rating System

Overall Score

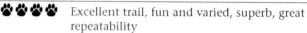

🐾🐾🐾🐾	Excellent trail, fun and varied, superb, great repeatability
🐾🐾🐾	Very good, lots to see for humans and K-9s, nice area
🐾🐾	Nice, possibly more fun for dogs than humans, usually easy going
🐾	Decent, mostly flat and not a terribly exciting walk, still off-leash.

Difficulty

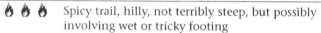

🔥🔥🔥	Spicy trail, hilly, not terribly steep, but possibly involving wet or tricky footing
🔥🔥	Moderate, varied terrain, good footing, could include crossing a bridge or stream
🔥	Mild, flat, not difficult, often paved, good for geriatric K-9s or humans.

Parking

🦴🦴🦴	Designated parking area away from traffic, maximum safety for unloading your pets; usually also includes an informational kiosk
🦴🦴	Medium-sized parking area, no more than three to four cars, but off pavement and safe for letting your dogs out of your vehicle
🦴	Very small or not even a designated parking area, could be alongside a road or only slightly off pavement. Not terribly safe for off-leash dogs to jump out of your vehicle, so please use caution when you load and unload your pets (if need be, put them on a leash until you get on the trail).

Trail Markings

★★★	Easy to follow tree markers; you can see the next marker from the previous one
★★	Some trail markings, but at times you may need to turn around to find the trail's direction; you may "lose" the trail for a bit
★	Intermittent markings on the trees, not easy to "find" the trail's direction; there may only be a few ATV signs, but the trail itself is easy to follow.

Top Ten List

Caution ⚠

This symbol means that the trail is officially an on-leash walk.

_____

Note: Some of the distances in the driving directions may be off by
0.2–0.4 miles.

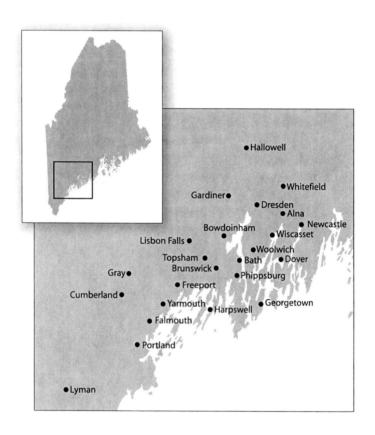

Contents—Walks Listed by Area

Contents

Lisbon/Lisbon Falls

Lyman

Newcastle

Phippsburg/Popham

Portland

Topsham

MAINE
Unleashed

Androscoggin River Bike Path (Topsham)

Overall Score	🐾🐾	Difficulty	🔥
Average Time	1 hr.	Parking	🦴🦴🦴
Average Distance	1–2 miles	Trail Markings	None

This is a unique and convenient location for a dog-walking area. The trails are not marked, but they are wide and well used and are not hard to follow. You will come down to a large ball field from the parking area, and you can cross it to get to more trails that run parallel to the river (or simply run around in this large, mown field!). I have met people with dogs off-leash here, but this place is by no means busy. The river you are walking parallel to is the Androscog-

gin River. It is good for swimming, but the current can be strong, so keep an eye on your pets. Several paths lead away from the large ball field. Most of these are out-and-backs, but two do make a circle. Some of the properties at the northeastern end of this place have "posted" signs. You will end up taking the same path back to your car from the large ball field. Please clean up after your pet. Poop bags are provided at the parking area, and the trash-cans are down by the ball field.

Directions: Located in a relatively populated area in Topsham. Take the first Topsham exit if you are coming from Bath on U.S. Route 1. Go north on Route 196 to the first lighted intersection (Route 196 and Route 24). Go right here, and then take the immediate next right, this is Middlesex Road. Go less than 0.1 mile and then turn left onto Foreside Road. Alternately, if you are coming north on Interstate 295, take Exit 31. The Exit says "Topsham/Route 196". Go south on Route 196, toward Brunswick. As you come down a long hill toward U.S. Route 1, go left on Middlesex Road, take the very next right, followed by the next immediate left, onto Foreside Road. Once on Foreside Road, head east for 0.4 (almost 0.5) miles. You will see the green "Androscoggin River Bike Path" sign on the right side of the road. The parking area for this dog walk is directly after the sign on the right. You will see a metal gate with the green "poop bag dispenser" hanging on it.

Austin Cary Lot (Harpswell)

Overall Score	🐾🐾	Difficulty	🔥
Average Time	45 min.	Parking	🦴
Average Distance	1–2.2 miles	Trail Markings	None

This is a 222-acre area that has a surplus of ATV and logging trails. There are beautiful views of Long Reach Cove. There is lots of water frontage of both Long Reach and Doughty Coves. This area is managed by Baxter State Park Authority and is used mostly for timber harvesting. This is

a very special property, because there are no restrictions, no signs, and no trail markers, and thus it is a spectacular place to take your pooches off-leash. You will have to find your own way here. Trailheads lead into the timber on the left and right sides of Long Reach Road (dirt road). Please respect ANY signs that say "private property or no trespassing," even if you encounter them out in the thickest, deepest woods. Such signs are posted for a reason, so please be responsible and turn around if you encounter such a posting. As always, enjoy yourself, take pictures, praise your dogs, and do not leave anything but paw prints behind. It's a good idea to bring a compass or GPS unit to help you keep your bearings.

Directions: Take U.S. Route 1 to the Cooks Corner exit and head south (straight through the large four-way intersection) on Route 24. Stay on Route 24 S for 4.9 (almost 5.0) miles. Make a right onto Long Reach Road. This is not easy to find; it will seem as though you are driving through the Harpwell's used-car lot. Long Reach Road is dirt and winds around to the left and then behind the car lot. Once you get onto Long Reach Road, you will immediately see the green Austin Cary Lot sign. The property begins here. After passing this green sign (it is on the right side of the road), you can start looking for places to park. There are small outcroppings that afford parking. You can also spot the "No ATVs" signs wherever there is a trailhead (on both sides of the road). Eventually you will cross over a small bridge, over a section of Long Reach Cove, and if you continue, there is a nice parking area on the right directly past the sign that reads "You are now leaving Austin Cary Lot." A trailhead starts here and will take you to a lovely place where your four-legged friends can safely swim and frolic in the water. It is quite shallow.

Back Bay (Green) Preserve (Birch Point, Bath)

Overall Score	🐾🐾🐾	Difficulty	🔥
Average Time	35–55 min.	Parking	One car
Average Distance	1.5 miles	Trail Markings	None

Very hard to find, but well worth the trouble. There are no markings on the trees, no trail maps, and virtually no parking area, but the trail is easy to follow and the view at the end of the trail where it meets the water is spectacular! There are a slew of fallen trees across the trail, so it becomes an obstacle course for you and your pooches. Some trees the dogs (and you) will go over and others they (not you) will crawl under, so the going is slow. The view at the end is straight out to the Atlantic Ocean. You can continue walking around to the left after you arrive at the water, but this trail ends at someone's private property, so please respect the small sign and turn around (going back the

same way you came). Please bring your own poop bags and clean up after your pets. It is 0.7 mile from where you park to the water's edge.

Directions: Take U.S. Route 1 to Bath and then take the High Street/Phippsburg exit. Go south on High Street for 2.5 miles. If you are coming from the north on U.S. Route 1, exit in Bath and turn left on Washington Street. Take Washington Street until it intersects with High Street and go left (south) on High Street for 0.6 mile. On your right will be the small Winnegance Store; veer right here. Do not follow Route 209 South; stay on the extension of High Street. After 1 mile (beyond the Winnegance Store) High Street turns into Campbell Pond Road; continue on Campbell Pond Road. Take a right onto Birch Point Road. The road will snake around the pond that is on the right. Follow Birch Point Road exactly 1 mile, then start looking to your left for a dark green sign that says "Birch Point Village Corporate Limits. No Hunting." About 40 feet after the dark green sign, you will see the one-car parking area (nose in first) and the trailhead. There is a fallen tree across the path. Go over this tree and continue across a wet area to get to the trail. Bring bug spray in the summer months.

Baker Forest (Newcastle)

Overall Score	🐾 🐾	Difficulty	🔥 🔥
Average Time	1–1.5 hrs.	Parking	🦴
Average Distance	1–2.5 miles	Trail Markings	★

This is a Damariscotta River Association property; it opened in 2003. Parts of the trails at this preserve run across private land, which is used by permission, so please be respectful. There are a variety of different trails to choose from, some marked and some not. I recommend staying on the trails that are marked. There is a lower and upper Blue Loop trail, an explorer trail (not marked), and a vernal pool. The trail starts out with quite an incline right from the parking area. The trails are at times narrow, and it is not always easy to

see the trail markings, because they are spaced out a bit far.
It may be a good idea to bring a compass or GPS unit. Maps
are sometimes available for the public, but not always.
The trail map is posted at the information kiosk, so you
can look at it before you start your walk to get an idea of
the shape of the property. The parking area is very close to
River Road, so please be careful when loading and unloading off-leash pooches. Bring your own poop bags and do
not remove anything from the woods.

Directions: Take U.S. Route 1 north from Brunswick
through Bath and over the bridge past Bath Iron Works
to Woolwich. Reset your mile counter on your car as you
come across the U.S. Route 1 Bridge into Woolwich. Continue north on U.S. Route 1 for a total of 15.3 (nearly 15.4)
miles. Some mile markers are as follows: After 8.6 miles
on U.S. Route 1 you will be in Wiscasset; continue over
a long bridge following signs toward Booth Bay. At 10.7
miles (from Woolwich) the large Sherman Lake Rest Area
is on the right side of the road. Continue going north on
U.S. Route 1. As you come to the 15.3-mile mark on your
odometer, a green sign with white script (on the right side
of the road) will indicate that you must go right to go to
Newcastle. Go right here; the road is called Sneed Spur.
Then go immediately right again (less than 0.1 mile) onto
River Road. (The sign will say Newcastle to the left and

Boothbay to the right; go right.) Stay on River Road for 1.1 miles. Baker Forest Preserve parking is on the right side of the road. A small gravel parking area is just off the pavement. You can see the information kiosk from River Road.

Basin Road and Fuller Mountain (Phippsburg)

Overall Score	🐾🐾🐾	Difficulty	🔥 🔥
Average Time	1–4 hrs.	Parking	Off-street
Average Distance	>2 miles	Trail Markings	★

This is a Nature Conservancy property. No official parking area or trail map exists as of yet. However, a large lot allows you to pull off Basin Road if you choose to take the walk that starts there. From this parking area, a trail has been created (as of Fall 2008). Light blue trail blazes are easy to see and follow. The trail starts

out as a very wide ATV type road and becomes a narrrow single file lane. It is an out and back walk, so when you get to the tree with the small white sign that says "Stay On Marked Trails"— turn around here. The entire walk will take about 1.5 to 2 hrs. Spots that are wet have 2 x 4s placed there for humans to use. Wear good footwear. Hunting is not allowed, but wear blaze orange in the fall anyway. Some additional trails across Basin Road to

the north are not marked, but are wide enough to allow you to find your way; to be safe, keep your bearings with a compass or GPS unit. This preserve is over 1100 acres, so you could be out here a while! Other trails off Meadowbrook have green and red signs that indicate whether ATVs are allowed or not. Many of these trails criss-cross and intersect. If you opt for the trailhead off the north side of

Basin Road, you will start out in dense woods, then cross a brook, and continue to climb up towards Fuller Mountain. There are deer here, so watch your pets if they tend to chase wildlife. This place can be used all year. You can also just walk on Basin Road itself, which is a dirt road, up from the water then down Hatch Road and looping back again onto Basin Road (very few cars).

Directions: From U.S. Route 1 North, take the High Street/ Phippsburg exit. Go right at the top of the ramp, heading south on Route 209 (High Street). Continue South on Route 209 for 5.6 (nearly 5.7) miles. Go right on Stoney Brook Road. Stay on this road for 1.5 miles; the road Ts with Meadowbrook Road. Go left at the T onto Meadowbrook Road. Stay on Meadowbrook Road for 1.5 miles. This is the end of the county-maintained road, so it turns to dirt. In the winter it is not plowed, so park right here. If you can drive further, continue another 0.3 mile, start looking to your left for "NO ATV" signs, then park on any gravel outcropping off the dirt road. Another trailhead can be found off Basin Road. You can take Basin Road off Route 209 South (1.3 miles further south from where Stoney Brook Road comes in from the right). Once on Basin Road, go 0.8 mile and park on the left side of the road. The trail starts here.

Basin Road intersects with Meadowbrook Road 1.3 miles from the turn off Route 209 S. After 1 mile on Basin Road, you will see a large rock with an American flag painted on it (on the right). Keep driving and you will come to the New Meadows River. There is easy access for dogs to swim here, and you can choose to park and walk from here as well.

Bass Falls Preserve (Alna)

Overall Score	🐾🐾🐾	Difficulty	🔥 🔥
Average Time	50 mins.	Parking	🦴 🦴
Average Distance	1.5 miles	Trail Markings	★ ★

This is a lovely 67-acre preserve owned by the Sheepscot Valley Conservation Association (SVCA). The trail starts out in a large field, where you follow a row of bird houses

along the edge of the field and into the woods. The tree blazes do not start up immediately as you come into the woods, so it can be a bit confusing. The map that is available is accurate in terms of what you might see and the general directions and layout of the trails, but the map's scale seems to be a bit underestimated (personal opinion). As you come down toward the Sheepscot River, you will have a choice of three trails (white, blue, red). There is easy water entry for a relaxing swim for water-loving dogs. It states in the free pamphlet: "Bass Falls is named in honor of the small waterfall that is seen at low tide and for the striped bass which live in the river." The preserve borders private property, so please keep your pets under control so they do not run onto private land. The parking area is quite small and grassy, so after a rainfall this area is practically under water. Plenty of roots stick up on the trail, so wear good shoes and watch your footing. Please bring your own poop bags and clean up after your pets. Sign the guestbook at the parking area—both you and your dogs.

Directions: Take U.S. Route 1 North from Brunswick through Bath and over the bridge past Bath Iron Works to Woolwich.

Reset the mile counter on your car as you come across the U.S. Route 1 Bridge into Woolwich. Continue north on U.S. Route 1 for 8.6 miles, and you will be in Wiscasset. In Wiscasset go left (north) on Route 218 N for 6.8 miles; you will travel toward Alna and then through Alna past the Alna Fire Station. The preserve is on the right side of the road; you will see the informational kiosk and the small grass parking area. Follow the bird houses to the right, away from your car.

Bath Off-leash Dog Park–
Washington Street Park (Bath)

Overall Score	🐾🐾🐾	Difficulty	Flat field
Average Time	15–40 mins.	Parking	🦴🦴🦴
Average Distance	0.3 mile	Trail Markings	None

This off-leash dog park is a large area, but it is not fenced in and there is no real boundary between the field and well-traveled Washington Street, so keep an eye on your canines. The large green field is bordered by the Kennebec River and Washington Street and has a great view of Bath Iron Works and the bridge to Woolwich. The park has a 0.3-mile gravel walking path that goes around the perimeter of the field, as well as two bocce ball courts and a dock. The park has a "poop bag" dispenser and a designated trash can for animal "waste" (no pun intended) near the parking area. There is access to the river for dogs to go swimming. Not all dogs are well socialized, so please watch your dogs closely while they interact with others. There is enough room here that you can play, run, and throw balls with your pets at the same time as other patrons do the same in a different

location; just be careful and alert. You are responsible for your pet's safety as well as that of other people and pets. Dog parks should be for socialization, not strictly for exercising. Your dogs should be exercised as normal before you take them to the park for a romp with other dogs.

Directions: Take U.S. Route 1 north to Bath and take the last (third) exit in Bath toward Historic Bath. Go down the hill to the first light and make a right by the post office. This is Washington Street. If you are coming south on U.S. Route 1 to Bath, come over the Kennebec Bridge and take the first exit in Bath. Continue straight down the hill to the first traffic light under the overpass and go left here. This is Washington Street. Once on Washington Street, go approximately 1.1 to 1.2 miles, and the park is on your left. There is a large paved parking area, which is kept cleared in the winter. Poop bags are in a dispenser mounted on a post near the silver trashcan that is for dog waste only.

Beatrice Baxter Memorial Forest (Topsham)

Overall Score	🐾🐾🐾	Difficulty	🔥
Average Time	1 hr.	Parking	Off street
Average Distance	2–3 miles	Trail Markings	None

This experimental forest is an enchanting place to take your off-leash pets. It has a single-file trail that starts to the right of the sign and disappears into the woods. After a bit the trail splits left and right. If you go left you will end up in a swampy area. Keep walking and the trail will eventually

loop back around the swamp and connect to the original trail. Bring bug spray in the summer and fall months.

Directions: Off U.S. Route 1, coming from either Brunswick or Bath, take the Topsham/Routes 196/24/201 exit. From Bath, this is the first exit for Topsham. Coming off the ramp, go 0.6 mile to the first light. Go right here. Take the next immediate right (Route 24 S) and then take the very next left; this is Foreside Road. Stay on Foreside Road for 3.6 miles. Go right on Pleasant Point Road. Stay on Pleasant Point Road for 0.9 mile, making sure to enjoy the views of the Androscoggin River on your right side; you will see the sign for the forest (pictured on the previous page) on the left side of the road. Proceed another 0.1 mile to a small outcropping, where you can park off the roadway (on the left). Walk back toward the large wooden sign; the small trail leads into the woods to the right of the sign. Bring bug spray, poop bags, leashes (just in case), and a compass or GPS unit.

Bijhouwer Forest Preserve (Phippsburg)

Overall Score	🐾🐾🐾	Difficulty	🔥🔥
Average Time	45 mins.	Parking	🦴🦴
Average Distance	1.5 miles	Trail Markings	★★★

A hidden gem. There are no trail maps, but they are unnecessary because of the easy-to-see tree blazes (blue). The trail is fairly wide and easy to follow. The trail makes a loop once you get down to the large open field (approximately 0.2 mile from the parking area). You can choose to go "straight" and thus counterclockwise around the loop or follow the trail around to the left (from the field) and go clockwise. As you enter this fabulous "forest," you will encounter several stream crossings. Boards are put down so you can safely cross; some dogs are not crazy about going across a foot-wide plank, so you may need to bring some treats to coax them across. Other dogs will choose to go through the water! Once you've made the trail's loop and you are back at the large field, you need to take the same

path back to your car. Bring your own poop bags and pick up after yourself and your four-legged friends.

Note: Because there is so much water and dampness in this dense forest, the mosquitoes are overpopulated. Bring a repellent for yourself and the dogs. Also, since the path takes you through a large, unmown field, be aware of ticks in the spring and summer.

Directions: Take U.S. Route 1 to Bath. Coming from the south on U.S. Route 1, get off at the second exit in Bath, High Street/Phippsburg, and go right at the top of the ramp. You are now on Route 209 S. Stay on Route 209 S for 6 (nearly 6.1) miles.

If you are coming into Bath from the north, exit U.S. Route 1 in Bath and follow the road under the overpass; you will see signs for Route 209 S. Go left on Washington Street, which intersects with Route 209 S after 2 miles. Go left onto Route 209 S and continue for 4.2 miles.

From this point go right on Stoney Brook Road (there is a big brick building on the corner). Stay on Stoney Brook Road for 0.6 miles. Slow down and look to your left; Devils Highway comes in from the left at the same moment that Stoney Brook Road veers to the right. There is a collection of mailboxes on the left side of the road. Go left onto Devils Highway and stay on it for 0.3 mile. The preserve parking is on your left. Devils Highway is a dirt road and quite pockmarked, so drive slowly. The parking area for this preserve is small but off the roadway. There is a green and yellow preserve sign and a gate.

Black Brook Preserve (Windham)

Overall Score	🐾🐾🐾	Difficulty	🔥
Average Time	1–2 hrs.	Parking	🦴🦴
Average Distance	1–3.5 miles	Trail Markings	★★

This is a fabulous property, owned and managed by Windham Land Trust. It is 105 acres in size and full of wildlife, great trails, and thick forest. Tree roots stick up from the earth in certain places along these trails and are very treacherous, so watch your footing. Be aware that the bugs are pretty thick during the summer and early fall months. This is a natural forested wetland, so after any amount of rainfall the parking area and the trails are very saturated (hint: wear rubber or waterproof boots or shoes). The trails are well marked, and at every trail intersection there is a wooden sign adorned with the trail map and an indicator of where you are now. You will cross or parallel two different brooks (especially along Hawkes Trail). Benches are built and placed along the trail for weary humans to sit on.

There are two different spots where you can park and access this trail system. The woods are dense, so if your dogs run off, call them back sooner rather than later. Bring your own poop bags and be respectful of other patrons by cleaning up your pets' waste. A compass or GPS unit is not necessary but is not a bad idea, since it is easy to get disoriented in a densely wooded area such as this. Hunting is permitted here, so wear blaze orange (your pets too) in the fall. Snowmobiles are allowed in the wintertime.

Directions: Take Interstate 295 South (if you are coming from Bath/Brunswick/Freeport or points further north or east) to Exit 11 (the Falmouth Connector to Interstate 95). Go south on I-95 to exit 48. Coming from the south, go north on I-95 to Exit 48. This is the Route 25/302–Riverside Street exit. Go north on Riverside Street for a little more than 1 mile (you will be traveling through a business-park area). Go left on Route 302 W. Stay on Route 302 W for 5.9 (nearly 6) miles. Go left on Albion Road and then take an immediate right onto Windham Center Road. Travel 1.1 miles on Windham Center Road and you will see the small parking area and sign for Black Brook Preserve on the right side of the roadway. Park close to the sign and study the map before you go, as there are no maps for the taking.

The secondary access area for this preserve is off Gray Road (a.k.a. Route 202/Route 4). If you come north on Route 202/4 from the Gorham area, the preserve is 0.3 mile north and on the right side of the road, north of the Route 202/4 intersection with Windham Center Road. If you are coming south on Route 202/4 from Gray, travel straight through the Fosters Corner roundabout, and the preserve is 0.4 (almost 0.5) mile further south on Route 202/4 on the left side. You can see the sign from Route 202/4 S.

Bliss Woods (Freeport)

Overall Score	🐾🐾	Difficulty	🔥
Average Time	45 mins.	Parking	🦴🦴
Average Distance	1–2 miles	Trail Markings	★★★

This is an easement on 87 acres of woodlands. It is sometimes used for forestry demonstrations for local school children, so small identification signs are mounted at the base of some of the trees. The trail is marked with yellow blazes and makes a loop. However, it is unclear from the map at the entrance to the parking area that this conservation area connects with the Sayles Field trail system, so it is easy to go too far. Thus, pay attention to the color of the blazes on the trees; when the blaze color switches from yellow to

white, you are heading toward Sayles Field. If you plan it that way, these two conservation properties can afford you hours of trails and dense woods to walk in. This property is fairly flat with some mild inclines, some wetlands, and lots of mosquitoes and horseflies (in the summer), so come prepared with bug spray. The parking area is off the paved road and has room for several vehicles. Bring your own poop bags and keep the woods clear of garbage. Do not remove anything from this forest. No formal map of these trails exists. This area was forested in the Fall of 2008, and is now a bit less dense in certain places along the trail.

Directions: Although the Bliss Woods and Sayles Field trails do connect, the directions are a bit different. To get to the Bliss Woods parking area, take Exit 20 off Interstate 295. Off the ramp head toward downtown Freeport, at the first light go right onto U.S. Route 1 South. Take the very next left, Pine Street. Travel on Pine Street for 1.4 miles until it comes to a four-way stop; take a right here onto S. Freeport Road. The entrance to this preserve will be on your right after traveling 1 mile on S. Freeport Road. If you are coming from the south on Interstate 295, take exit 17 and then go north on U.S. Route 1 toward Freeport. Go right on S. Freeport Road. The entrance to Bliss Woods will be on your left after traveling 0.5 mile on S. Freeport Road. Take a look at the rudimentary map on the sign as you drive in to park.

Bowdoin College Athletic Fields (Brunswick)

Overall Score	🐾🐾	Difficulty	Flat field
Average Time	>1 hr.	Parking	🦴🦴🦴
Average Distance	0.25 miles	Trail Markings	None

This is a great place to go for off-leash socialization on the weekends. On Saturday and Sunday mornings many dog owners bring their pets here and let them romp around on the athletic fields. You must bring your own poop bags and water, since they will get very thirsty from playing. Most dogs who come here are very well socialized. You are ultimately responsible for your own and others' safety. The best time to go is between 9AM and 12 noon.

Directions: You will need to get to Brunswick, either from I-295 (Exit 28) or U.S. Route 1 from Bath (or Topsham). Go to the intersection of Bath Road and Route 123 S (toward Harpswell). You can do this by driving toward Bowdoin College from downtown Brunswick and then going left on Bath Road, or you can take the Cooks Corner exit off U.S. Route 1 coming south and then go right onto Bath Road at the Cooks Corner intersection (first light after the off ramp). At the intersection of Route 123 and Bath Road (by Bowdoin College), go south on Route 123. After 0.5 mile the Bowdoin Athletic Field entrance and sign will be on your right. Park near the brick complexes (dead ahead as you turn into the parking lot) and then walk around to the fields in back of these buildings.

Bowdoin College Coastal Studies Center (Orr's Island)

Overall Score	🐾🐾	Difficulty	🔥🔥
Average Time	1–2 hrs.	Parking	🦴🦴🦴
Average Distance	1.4–4 miles	Trail Markings	★★★

This area is frequented mostly on the weekends and mostly by people without dogs. There are a total of seven different trails to choose from. If you walk the perimeter of all of them, you have covered in excess of 3.85 miles. Please observe the signs posted by the college and do not tread off the marked trails. There is a farm road and orchards, as well as shore trails to explore. This is an active research facility, and there are researchers in residence. The free map available at the parking kiosk is quite accurate and to scale, so utilize it in order to stay on the trails. As mentioned, most of the people who come here do not bring dogs, so please be courteous and respectful of other patrons. Poop bags are provided at the parking area. This is a 118-acre property. Most of the trails do end up with a lovely view of Harpswell Sound, Long Cove, or Wyer Island and Dogs Head. One can walk out to Wyer Island during low tide, where swimming is a must for those water-loving dogs.

Note: It does state that dogs should be on a leash while on these trails, but let it be known that I have met people with their pets off-leash here. You will have to make your own decision when you visit this property.

Directions: Take Interstate 295 North from Portland to Exit 28, Brunswick/U.S. Route 1. Travel through Brunswick and pick up U.S. Route 1 North to Cooks Corner. Exiting at Cooks Corner, follow the signs for Route 24 South. If you are coming south on U.S. Route 1, come through Bath

and then exit at Cooks Corner. Go straight through the first large traffic-light intersection, following the signs for Route 24 S. Stay on Route 24 S for a little over 11 miles. You will come to a rise in the road, and the road will curve slightly to the left; here Bay View Road will come in from your right. Go right on Bay View Road and stay on it until it ends (approximately 0.9 mile). The Bowdoin College Coastal Studies Center is located at 240 Bay View Road on Orr's Island. Park near the green and brown informational sign. Do not drive all the way in to the farmhouse.

Bradbury Mountain State Park (Freeport/Pownal Center)

Honorable Mention

As with most state parks, you have to pay a daily fee. There are many trails here and dogs are allowed, but they must be leashed. This park is open all year. There is a free map, and the trails are well marked and often tended to. Bradbury Mountain is 485 feet above sea level, and the park is over 600 acres in size. There are picnic tables, a children's playground, a 41-acre campground, and several places to barbeque. There is no attendant during the off-season, which is between Labor Day and Memorial Day, and the honor system is assumed with respect to paying the park fee.

Directions: This Park is only 10 minutes from Freeport, and directional signs are widespread and can even be seen off Interstate 295 in both directions. Take Exit 22 off Interstate 295 and go west on Pownal Road, which becomes Elmwood Road. At the intersection of Elmwood Road and Route 9 (a.k.a. Hallowell Road) go right, and the park entrance is 0.5 mile up on your left.

Bruce Hill (North Yarmouth)

Overall Score	🐾🐾	Difficulty	🔥🔥
Average Time	1–1.5 hrs.	Parking	🦴
Average Distance	1–2.5 miles	Trail Markings	None

There are two main loop trails, each approximately 1.3 miles long and each taking about 40 minutes to complete. However, these loops do intersect with other trails, and you can end up going further and spending more time in these woods than you may have planned. In the summertime the horseflies are horrible. Bruce Hill is a 76-acre land preserve that leads up to a 77-foot-tall Federal Avia-

tion Administration tower. Some of the trails are a bit muddy, and they are not marked. But the trails are at least 4 feet wide and well traveled, so there is really no need for markers. There is no official trail map, so it may be a good idea to bring a compass or GPS unit. Power lines bisect the property, and under the power lines are snowmobile trails that can also be utilized for walking. There are some large rocks in the trails, as well as ruts, sticks, and some steepish ascents and descents. Poison ivy has been spotted off the trails, so be careful if you venture off into the woods. Horse droppings were prevalent on many of the trails, so keep an eye out for equestrians. Please bring your own poop bags and clean up after your pets. Bring clean water for your dogs even if you just keep it in the car and give it to them after your walk; there is only minimal swamp water for drinking (or cooling off).

Directions: This property is in North Yarmouth, but is a Town of Cumberland property easement (preserve). From Interstate 295 take Exit 17, Yarmouth/U.S. Route 1. Go south on U.S. Route 1 for 0.9 mile (toward the center of Yarmouth). Go right on Main Street, a.k.a. Route 115 North. Stay on Route 115 N for 4.4 (almost 4.5) miles. Some landmarks are as follows: after 3.6 miles, Route 115 intersects with Route 9. Another 0.2 mile after this intersection Route 115 N veers left and Route 9 N continues straight. Keep going 0.6 mile after this fork (veering left); then go left on Henry Road. Stay on Henry Road for a total of 0.5 mile. After 0.3 mile Henry Road becomes dirt. Veer left at the fork in the road once it has turned to dirt. You will be going uphill; when you see the metal gate, park on the right side and then walk from here (up the road to the FAA tower). The trails will start from the tower area; one trail starts from the east side and the other on the west side of the fence surrounding the tower.

Brunswick to Cooks Corner Walking and Bike Path (Brunswick)

Overall Score	🐾 🐾	Difficulty	🔥
Average Time	1–2 hrs.	Parking	🦴 🦴 🦴
Average Distance	1–7.5 miles	Trail Markings	None

This is primarily an on-leash walk, but I have met others here with well-behaved dogs off-leash. It is a paved "trail" that goes from the Cooks Corner area to Brunswick and is about 3.5 miles long (in one direction). People bike, Rollerblade, walk with baby carriages, jog, walk or run with their pets, and speed-walk here at all times of year. The road is plowed and sanded in the wintertime. It runs parallel to U.S. Route 1, so the traffic noise can be stifling. But in inclement weather or when the ice is treacherous on the trails in the woods it is a nice place to exercise your dogs. Poop bags are provided at both ends, and trash dispensers can be found along the way. Be diligent about cleaning up after your dogs. Bring your leashes on this walk and respect other patrons.

Directions: This path can be picked up from the Brunswick entrance or the Cooks Corner area. To get to the Brunswick entrance, you must get to Federal Street. Take I-295 or U.S. Route 1 to downtown Brunswick; Maine Street is the "main" street in this town. Parallel to Maine Street on the east side is Federal Street. Federal Street runs north to south. Take Federal Street north and cross over the U.S. Route 1 (North) on-ramp. Federal Street now becomes Water Street. Take Water Street all the way to the end. Here there is a large paved parking area for the walking path.

To get to the Cooks Corner entrance near the round church, exit U.S. Route 1 at Cooks Corner and go left onto Bath Road (at the first lighted intersection). Go to the second light (you will see Lowe's on your right) and take a left onto Old Bath Road (also called Old Brunswick Road). Go over the bridge (over railroad tracks) and then start to slow down, because you will be making a sharp left after the bridge, onto Grover Lane. You will see the green sign for the bike path on the left side of the road. Go to the very end of Grover Lane (about. 0.4 mile) and park here (on the left). The round church is on your right. You can park in the church lot if there are no spaces on the left.

Brunswick Town Commons (Brunswick)

Overall Score	🐾 🐾	Difficulty	🔥
Average Time	1–2 hrs.	Parking	🦴🦴
Average Distance	1–4 miles	Trail Markings	★

The trails are wide, and there are signs periodically throughout the trail system showing you where to go, but there are no formal trail markings. Even though this trail system is utilized in all seasons, it is very, very easy to get disoriented and "lost"—so please remember your Boy or Girl Scout tricks of how to find your way in the woods or bring a GPS unit or compass. Many people use this park, so you will often meet others on foot or on a mountain bike. There is a strict leash law in the town of Brunswick, so it is a very good idea to leash your dogs when you are near the parking area. I have run into a Forest Ranger on a mountain bike in the woods here and was told to put my dogs on a

leash immediately. However, the majority of people who utilize this place have their dogs off-leash, and usually there are no Forest Rangers or Animal Control persons about. Please do bring your own poop bags and pick up after your pets. It is a densely wooded area, so mosquitoes are rampant in the summertime. Houses are all around the perimeter of the entire Town Commons (which encompasses nearly 80 acres), so if you truly get lost you will eventually get to a road or home.

Directions: You will need to get to Brunswick, either from I-295 (Exit 28) or U.S. Route 1 from Bath (or Topsham). Go to the intersection of Bath Road and Route 123 South (toward Harpswell). You can do this by driving toward Bowdoin College from downtown Brunswick and then going left on Bath Road; or you can take the Cooks Corner exit off U.S. Route 1 coming south and then go right onto Bath Road at the Cooks Corner intersection (first light after the off-ramp). At the intersection of Route 123 and Bath Road (by Bowdoin College), go south on Route 123. After 1.5 (very nearly 1.6) miles the town-commons sign and parking lot will appear on your right. There are other places to enter into this trail system, but this is the best place to park.

Butler Head Preserve (North Bath)

Overall Score	🐾🐾🐾	Difficulty	🔥🔥
Average Time	50 mins.–1 hr.	Parking	🦴
Average Distance	1.5–2 miles	Trail Markings	★

This area is fairly remote, but it is a really nice hour-long walk with lots to see, smell, and chase! It used to be a cross-country-skiing area, so some of the trails are wide and marked with white blazes on the trees. However, the trail markings have faded in many places and some trails have become overgrown, so I recommend simply staying on the better-trodden ones. From where you park, one trail leads directly into a large field; in the summer it is infested with ticks, so be aware. To avoid going through this field,

continue up the dirt road (Butler Head Road) to Mallard Road (coming in from the left). Enter the woods here and you can pick up another trail on the left, essentially where Mallard Road dead-ends. This trail will eventually loop back around to the large field and your vehicle; this loop is about 1.75 miles long. This preserve encompasses 133 acres of woods. Please obey the private-property signs posted by people who own camps in this area.

Directions: Take U.S. Route 1 to Bath and the High Street/ Phippsburg exit. At the top of the ramp go left (north) onto High Street. If you are coming from the north, exit U.S. Route 1 as you come into Bath and go straight down a small hill to the first light. Go right here; this is Washington Street. At the next light go left onto Center Street, then up another hill to High Street. At High Street go right. From either direction, stay on High Street for 1.5 miles. Go left on Whiskeag Road. Stay on Whiskeag Road 1.1 miles; it merges with Oak Grove Avenue. Go right onto N. Bath Road and stay on this road for 1.5 miles. Go right on Varney Mill Road. After 0.6 (nearly 0.7) mile on Varney Mill Road look to your left for a dirt road. This dirt road has a sign that says "Dead End"; this is Butler Head Road.

Go left here. After 0.1 mile on Butler Head Road you will see a large sign with the information box. You can pick up a map here, but beware: This map is utterly useless in terms of viewing trails or getting your bearings. Continue on for 0.1 mile and park on the right. There will be water, Merrymeeting Bay, on your right. The parking area is small and can probably only accommodate three cars.

Calderwood Preserve (Freeport)

Overall Score	🐾🐾	Difficulty	🔥
Average Time	25–55 mins.	Parking	Off-roadway
Average Distance	1.4 miles	Trail Markings	★★

This preserve encompasses 50 acres, but it is divided into two parts on either side of a fairly busy paved road. The trails that lead away from the road (Flying Point Road) are both marked and easy to follow. The trail that goes down to Maquoit Bay makes a loop, while its counterpart across the street is an out and back. You can see the water in the bay, but you are fairly high up and away from the water's edge, so there really is no water access. The out-and-back trail is longer and you end up at a swamp, which is probably why this trail is quite wet in places. Unfortunately, there is no designated parking area or informational kiosk, so you have to simply pull off the pavement as best you can. The lack of parking so close to a busy road always makes me nervous with off-leash dogs, so please be very careful. You may even want to leash your pets until you are well into the woods. It is a pretty area, and the woods are very peaceful and green.

Directions: Take Interstate 295 north or south to Exit 20 in Freeport. Travel on Lower Main Street and then Main Street into the center of town. As you see the L.L. Bean flagship store on your left, go right onto Bow Street. This road will change names, and eventually (after about 1 mile) you will be on Flying Point Road. Stay on Flying Point Road for another 4.1 miles. (From the turn onto Bow Street in Freeport Center, you will travel 5.1 miles.) The preserve is on both sides of the road. Very small signs only a few feet off the roadway indicate that you have arrived at the Calderwood Preserve. I recommend turning around and parking off the road with your car's nose headed back toward Freeport; the shoulder is a bit wider in this direction. Be very careful with yourself and your pets so near traffic.

Capisic Pond Park (Portland)

Overall Score	🐾🐾	Difficulty	🔥
Average Time	>20 mins.	Parking	🦴
Average Distance	1 mile	Trail Markings	None

An unofficial off-leash park in the middle of a densely populated area. Lots of grass to run on, benches for humans to sit on; ducks can be seen swimming in the pond, and there are wooden man-made bridges that allow you to cross a brook that runs into the pond. This park is a nice refuge

for humans and pets. People seem to come here to actually walk with their dogs off-leash rather than stand around and watch the dogs play. Bring your own poop bags and clean up after your pets. This park is not fenced. There are homes lining both sides of the park. The main trail (or walking path) runs the length of the property, with the pond on one side and grassy areas or private yards on the other. This is an out-and-back walk, because once you've walked the length of the path (about 0.5 mile), you have to turn around and go back the same way. Near the small parking area the property is a bit wider and larger.

Directions: From Interstate 295 in Portland take Exit 5B, Congress Street, and start heading toward the airport (west). Take a right at the first sizable intersection; this is Stevens Avenue. Travel about 100 feet, then go left onto Capisic Street. The park is ahead on the right. You will probably see Capisic Pond before you actually see Macy Street on your right (where you will be parking). If you cross the bridge that goes over the pond, you will have to turn around and go back. Macy Street is a very small and a short dead-end street. Drive down Macy Street to the gate that leads into the park. You will see a brown and white sign that identifies Capisic Pond Park. Park here. It is a very small parking area, and you will have to park either nose in or turn around in the nearby driveway and back up to the gate leading into the park.

Center Pond Preserve (Phippsburg)

Overall Score	🐾🐾🐾🐾	Difficulty	🔥🔥🔥
Average Time	1–3 hrs.	Parking	🦴🦴🦴
Average Distance	1–4.7 miles	Trail Markings	★★★

The trails are well marked and well kept. This is varied terrain, with lots of fresh water to swim in, and a safe parking area. You can pick up a trail map at the parking area; the map is accurate and in ample supply. There is a Perimeter Trail that is 4.7 miles long, marked with blaze

orange paint on the trees. However, you do not have to go the entire loop; other trails create shorter, concentric circles within the Perimeter Trail. There are 253 acres at your disposal here. There are some wider logging roads that intersect with other narrower trails, and you do have to cross a brook on a man-made bridge (not always popular with dogs). Some trail intersections have the map stapled to a tree so you can get your bearings. This is an easily accessible and very usable preserve. Dogs can swim in Beaver Pond or Center Pond and there are stone walls,

viewpoints, old house foundations, and wetlands to look at and explore. There are some wet spots and mud on the trails, so bring good footwear. Mosquitoes are rampant in the summer months. As always, please clean up after your pets and carry out anything you bring in with you.

Directions: Take U.S. Route 1 to Bath. Coming from the south on U.S. Route 1, get off at the second exit in Bath, High Street/Phippsburg, and go right at the top of the ramp. This is Route 209 S. Stay on Route 209 S for 6.8 miles. If you are coming into Bath from the north, exit U.S. Route 1 in Bath and follow the road under the overpass; you will see signs for Route 209 S. Go left on Washington Street, which intersects with Route 209 S after 2 miles. Go left onto Route 209 S and continue for 5 miles. Whichever direction you are coming from, Parker Head Road comes in from the left. You will see a sign for the town library and the 1774 Inn B&B (pointing to the left). You will have the Bisson Center Store on your right. Go left here. Stay on Parker Head Road for 0.5 mile. The parking area and sign for Center Pond Preserve (dark green with white letters) will be on your right. Maps are in the little box below the preserve sign.

Chaffin Pond Trail/Preserve (North Windham)

Overall Score	🐾🐾🐾🐾	Difficulty	🔥 🔥
Average Time	30–55 mins.	Parking	🦴🦴
Average Distance	1–1.9 miles	Trail Markings	★

A spectacular place to go with dogs. A freshwater pond, several trails to choose from, a good parking area, and some neat man-made bridges. The trail markers come in the form of arrows that are stapled to trees whenever the trail changes direction. The problem is that these arrows are mounted in one direction, assuming that walkers will all be coming around the lake in the counterclockwise direction. So at times you may need to look behind you (especially at trail intersections) to determine where you want to go. The trails are well trampled and easy to follow. Some areas are quite wet, so bring good footwear. The pond is beautiful and can be entered in several different locations. Please bring your own poop bags and clean up after your pets.

Directions: You have to get to Route 302 West out of Portland. There are several ways to do this—the easiest may be via Exit 48 off I-95 North or South. Follow the signs for Route 302 (you will be on Riverside Street (going north) for about a mile after you come off I-95). Once you are on Route 302 West, you will travel a total of 11.3 (a little more) miles, and Chaffin Pond Preserve is on the right. A small sign is visible off 302 W as you go through N. Windham. Mile-markers are as follows: at 5.9 miles on Route 302 W you'll pass Albion Road; at 7.4 miles you will come to a large roundabout representing the intersection of Routes 302/202/4; at 10 miles you will come to the intersection of Routes 35 and 115. A short dirt road off Route 302 W leads down to the small parking area.

Cousins River Trail (Freeport)

Overall Score	🐾🐾🐾	Difficulty	🔥 🔥
Average Time	1–1.5 hrs.	Parking	🦴🦴
Average Distance	1–2.5 miles	Trail Markings	★★

This preserve is jointly managed by the Freeport YMCA, the Cousins River easement, and the Powell Point Freeport Conservation Trust. There are three main trails at your

disposal, and you will end up by the Cousins River, where water-loving dogs can take a dip. The trail starts uphill and then goes into the woods and becomes less strenuous. The tree markings are clear, and elevated walkways have been installed where there is mud or a wet area. Dogs are allowed off leash here, but you must clean up after your pet (so bring bags for pet waste). The mosquitoes can be a problem in the summer months, so bring

YMCA - COUSINS RIVER PRESERVE TRAIL SYSTEM

your bug spray. As you come up the hill from the YMCA, you will intersect with the Lambert Road trail, which takes you over a crest and down to the road, adding an out-and-back jaunt of about 0.65 mile to your walk. The remainder of the trail (marked by white tree blazes) takes you down to the river.

Directions: Take Interstate 295 to Freeport to Exit 17, Yarmouth/Freeport. Go north on U.S. Route 1 for 1.1 miles. Turn right onto Old Freeport Road; the YMCA is on the top of the hill to your right. Pull into the parking area and drive all the way to the back left corner of this lot, where you will see the informational kiosk and trailhead heading up and away from the parking area. (The YMCA building will be to your right.) There are no free maps, but take a look at the map posted at the trailhead to get your bearings and to see the trail's orientation. Bringing a compass or GPS unit is not a bad idea.

Cox Pinnacle (Durham/Brunswick)

Overall Score	🐾🐾🐾	Difficulty	🔥 🔥
Average Time	45 mins.–1 hr.	Parking	🐾 🐾
Average Distance	0.8–1.4 miles	Trail Markings	★★★

A fun, short jaunt to the top of Cox Pinnacle. I believe this to be a well-utilized park, because the trails are always well trampled throughout the year. Incredibly, I have yet to actually meet another human or dog while walking this small collection of hiking trails. These are very easy-to-follow trail markings: blue wooden pieces nailed to the trees. There are several trails that all lead up to the pinnacle, where someone has erected a small stone pyramid (pile of rocks). If you follow the trail marked "Durham Road," you will end up in a different location than where you parked, but it's still a nice walk. You simply have to turn around and go back the same way. The walk up to the pinnacle can be made into a loop. Please pick up after yourself and your animals—poop bags are not provided.

I have spotted horse manure on these trails, so keep a look out for the possibility of meeting horses (hopefully with their riders!).

Note: This is a Town of Brunswick Park. The Town of Brunswick has a leash-law policy, so it may be a good idea to leash your dogs as you depart from and approach the parking area.

Directions: Take U.S. Route 1 or Interstate 295 to Brunswick. If coming from the south, take I-295 North to Exit 28 and look for signs for U.S. Route 1 South, which is a right-hand turn off the ramp. If you are coming from Bath, drive through Brunswick on U.S. Route 1 South and follow the signs to Interstate 295. As you get onto the I-295 ramp, stay in the left lane. Look for the signs indicating U.S. Route 1 South. Take a hard left, nearly a 180-degree turn from the I-295 on-ramp, onto the I-295 off-ramp. This is a bit tricky, so drive carefully. Immediately merge over to the far right-hand lane and then turn right onto U.S. Route 1 South. Go 0.6 mile on U.S. Route 1 S, then take the first right, Durham Road. Stay on Durham Road for 3 miles. Next take Hacker Road right. (The road is named Collinsbrook Road if you incorrectly go left here.) After 0.2 mile on Hacker Road you will see the Cox Pinnacle (dark green with gold writing) sign on your left indicating the parking area.

Cumberland Town Forest (Cumberland)

Overall Score	🐾🐾	Difficulty	🔥
Average Time	1–1.5 hrs.	Parking	🦴🦴🦴
Average Distance	1.5–3 miles	Trail Markings	★★

Here you can follow an ancient Freedom Trail or a Self-Guided Nature Trail. You will actually be visiting a place where early revolutionaries fought. A 1.5-mile trail runs along the perimeter of this 75-acre park. Wooden bridges help you cross streams and wet areas. It is a damp trail, so mosquitoes love this place in the summer months. According to the Town of Cumberland web site, "Wooden benches and informational kiosks honor soldiers of the revolutionary war and allow you to sit and reflect. The self-guided tour has 16 stops, and teaches you about forest ecology and biological diversity. Boy Scouts from Troop 58 originally created this trail. Several different kinds of pine can be seen here." Dogs are allowed off-

leash on voice command. Please bring your own poop bags and clean up after your pets. The trail markings are quite faded, but the trail is wide and easy to follow. If no maps are available, you will have to memorize the trail layout at the information kiosk.

Directions: Take Exit 15 off Interstate 295, looking for signs for U.S. Route 1 South. Take U.S. Route 1 South and after 0.9 (almost 1) mile, go left, then immediately right, and you will be on a bridge that brings Tuttle Road over U.S. Route 1. If you go under this bridge (on U.S. Route 1 South), you will have to turn around and go back. After getting onto Tuttle Road, go 2.4 (nearly 2.5) miles, and the Cumberland Town Offices are on your left. Turn into the Town Offices and park near the rear, left-hand side of the parking area. The informational kiosk is visible from the parking area. The trailhead starts right here.

Dodge Point (Newcastle)

Overall Score	🐾🐾	Difficulty	🔥 🔥
Average Time	45 mins.–2 hrs.	Parking	🦴 🦴 🦴
Average Distance	1–3 miles	Trail Markings	★

This is a very popular and busy property, especially with dog people. Most everyone allows their pets to run off-leash here. There are several trails to choose from, but not all are equally well marked. Those trails that are marked seem to have intermittent blazes on the trees, so a compass or GPS unit would not be a bad idea. There is a map of the property posted on the informational kiosk near the parking area, but every time I have been to this property no maps were available for the public to take along. The Old Farm Road trail is wide and easy to follow and offers an interpretive path. The Shore trail goes down to the water and has some beautiful views of the Damariscotta River. The property actually has over 8000 feet of river frontage. The Ravine trail has some high roots that stick up, so be careful of your footing. This place is open and utilized for hiking, dog walking, and mountain biking all year. Bring your

own poop bags and clean up after your pets. Keep in mind that you are responsible for your pets' behavior (so bring leashes).

Directions: Take U.S. Route 1 North from Brunswick through Bath and over the bridge past Bath Iron Works to Woolwich. Reset your mile counter on your car as you come across the U.S. Route 1 bridge into Woolwich. Continue north on U.S. Route 1 for a total of 15.3 (nearly 15.4) miles. Some mile markers are as follows: After 8.6 miles on U.S. Route 1 you will be in Wiscasset; you will continue over a long bridge following signs toward Booth Bay (without turning southward). Continue on U.S. Route 1 through Edgecomb. At 10.7 miles (from Woolwich) a large rest area, the Sherman Lake Rest Area, is on the right side of the road. As you come to the 15.3-mile mark, a green sign with white letters will indicate that you must go right in order to go to Newcastle (similarly, a blue sign with white writing says "Newcastle Marine"). Go right here; the road is called Sneed Spur. Then go immediately right again (less than 0.1 mile) onto River Road. Stay on River Road for 2.3 miles. The Dodge Point preserve is on your left. The parking area is dirt.

Dundee Park (South Windham)

Seasonable-Honorable Mention

No pets are allowed at this property when the park is open between Memorial Day and Labor Day, but when the park is closed you can bring your furry friends and enjoy the space. There are 20 acres at your disposal here on the shores of the Presumpscot River. There are picnic tables, benches, a volleyball court, a basketball court, and a sandy

beach. There are no trails per se, but it is a good open place for dogs to run around and perhaps go swimming. The current in the river can at times be severe, so keep an eye on those water-loving dogs. Clean up after your pet even though the park is closed for the season.

Directions: This park is located northwest of Portland. You can take Exit 48 off Interstate 95 and follow the signs to Route 25 West (you might be on Route 25 Business for a bit); then pick up Route 237 West toward South Windham. Once you get to the intersection of Routes 202 N and 237 W (there is a roundabout here), go north on Route 202/4 for about 1 mile. Go left on River Road and travel approximately 5 miles. Dundee Road comes in from the left. Go left onto Dundee Road and travel to the end of it. You can also come down Route 202 to the intersection of Routes 202/4 and 302. Continue south on Route 202/4 for 0.7 mile, then go right on Windham Center Road. Proceed until Windham Center Road intersects with River Road and go left (south) on River Road. Dundee Road comes in from the right; go right and to the end of Dundee Road. The park is at the end of the road. If the gate is open, you can drive in; if not you can park by the gate and walk to the beach area.

Echo-Two Trails (Brunswick)

Overall Score	🐾🐾🐾	Difficulty	🔥 🔥
Average Time	1.5–2 hrs.	Parking	🦴
Average Distance	2–3 miles	Trail Markings	★ ★

Park your vehicle in the same space as for the Cox Pinnacle trail system and leave the parking lot to your left down Hacker Road—toward a lone white house that is across the street. Walk approximately 125 to 150 feet. Cross the street so that you now are on the same side as the lone white house; if you turn around, you will see the Cox Pinnacle sign behind you on the opposite side of the road. Look into the woods, up a small incline; there are blue mark-

ers (blazes) on the trees. This is the trailhead. Start climbing up and away from Hacker Road—the white house is now directly on your right.

The trail zigzags a bit, but it is easy to follow the tree blazes. The trail will eventually split left and right. If you go to the left, you will drop down into a large field and out into open terrain. Going to the right, you will stay on the trail system and continue through the woods. You will come upon several trail intersections, and the color of the trail markers will change.

There are three main trails: orange, blue, and red. The red and orange trails intersect near Woods Road, and if you continue south on Woods Road for 0.5 mile you will get to White's Beach (a campground and lake). All in all the trails are well marked. A few spots require river crossings; 2 x 4s are laid down. There is no official information kiosk or trail map, so keep your bearings and stay on the marked trails. Bringing a compass or GPS system is not a bad plan. The only way back to your vehicle is the same way you came into this trail system (off Hacker Road).

Note: Please do put your dogs on a leash until you get to the trails, because Hacker Road is very busy and dangerous. This trail system "belongs" to the Echo-Two community. Several of the trails run very close to some of the homes in this community. If you have dogs (like mine) that like to go into people's yards to chase cats, this walk may not be ideal. However, if your dogs are better at staying on the trails and want to be challenged by rolling hills and switchback turns, then this is a good place.

Directions: Take U.S. Route 1 or Interstate 295 to Brunswick. If you are coming from the south, take I-295 north to Exit 28 and look for signs for U.S. Route 1 South, which is a right-hand turn off the exit ramp. If you are coming from Bath, drive through Brunswick on U.S. Route 1 and follow the signs to Interstate 295. As you get onto the I-295 ramp, stay in the left lane. Look for the signs indicating U.S. Route 1 South. Take a hard left, nearly a 180-degree turn from the I-295 on-ramp, onto the I-295 off-ramp. This is a bit tricky, so drive carefully. Immediately merge over to the far right lane and then turn right onto U.S. Route 1 South. Go 0.6 mile on U.S. Route 1 South and then take the first right, Durham Road. Stay on Durham Road for 3 miles. Take Hacker Road right; the road is named Collinsbrook Road if you incorrectly go left here. After 0.2 mile on Hacker Road you will see the Cox Pinnacle (dark green with gold writing) sign on your left, indicating the parking area.

Edgecomb to Ward Road (Lisbon Falls and Topsham)

Overall Score	🐾🐾	Difficulty	🔥
Average Time	1–3 hrs.	Parking	🦴
Average Distance	2–7 miles	Trail Markings	None

A vast expanse of dirt roads, ATV trails, and narrow, woodsy trails. The best walking is on the road, but the ATV trails are well used, so they give you some more options. This area is a mix of private properties, State of Maine

Inland Fisheries property, and open spaces. Please observe the private or posted signs. After rainfall this area gets saturated and the road is wet, so wear good shoes. There are lots of possibilities at this location, but you may want to bring a compass or GPS unit.

Directions: This place can be accessed from two directions. The dirt road does go through, but it is very rocky, rutted, muddy, and narrow, so unless you have a super 4 x 4, I would drive in and out the same way. If you are coming from the north, take Interstate 95 to exit 80 and travel south on Route 196 to Lisbon and Lisbon Falls. Go left on Route 125 (Main Street) in Lisbon Falls. Go 1 mile, then go right onto Edgecomb Road. After 0.7 mile the road will turn to dirt. Keep going until you've traveled 1 to 1.5 miles and park off the roadway. Start walking from here, continuing on Edgecomb Road (which becomes Ward Road eventually). The ATV trails come in from both sides.

Coming from the south, take Interstate 295 North to Topsham (take exit 31) or U.S. Route 1 in Brunswick to Route 196 West. From the Route 196 and Interstate 295 intersection go about 1.5 miles west on Route 196. Go right on Meadow Cross Road. Stay on Meadow Cross Road for 1.9 miles and then go left on Ward Road. The pavement ends after 1 mile on Ward Road; continue another 0.5 mile up Ward Road and then park somewhere off the roadway and start walking. The road becomes rutted and narrow, and ATV trails will enter from both sides. You can stay on this dirt road or take one of the single tracks.

You can also take Route 201 North out of Topsham. Go 1.1 miles, then turn left onto Meadows Road. Go 1.9 miles down Meadows Road, then left onto Ward Road. After 1.5 miles Ward Road will get very narrow, rutted, and rocky, so I recommend parking off the roadway here.

Elbow Hill (Southwest Bath)

Overall Score	🐾🐾	Difficulty	🔥 🔥
Average Time	50 mins.–1 hr.	Parking	🦴
Average Distance	2 miles	Trail Markings	None

This place is fairly easy to find, but the trails are not all that intuitive and are not marked, so bring a compass or a GPS unit. Start walking straight ahead from where you park your vehicle through the new growth of pine trees. Take the second trail on the right. Stay on this trail until you get to a dirt road. Go left on the dirt road; this is

Sabino Road. You can walk on this road all the way to Houghton Pond. Houghton Pond will be visible through the trees on your right. The last street on the left indicates that you need to turn around; it is identified by a sign on a tree that says "Belmont." You will walk back on this peaceful and quiet dirt road and take the same trail back to your car. These are ATV and logging trails, so they are wide and fairly easy to follow. (In late summer they can get a bit overgrown.) The mosquitoes and ticks can be bad here from June to August. Set your compass/GPS unit before you randomly set out into these woods between Houghton Pond and Elbow Hill. You are relatively guaranteed not to meet anyone else, but residents may come driving along Sabino Road.

Directions: Take the High Street/Phippsburg exit in Bath off of U.S. Route 1 North. Go right or south off the ramp onto Route 209 South. Stay on this road for 2.6 miles. If you are coming south on U.S. Route 1 to Bath, come over the Kennebec Bridge and take the first exit in Bath. Continue straight down the hill to the first traffic light under the overpass and go left here. This is Washington Street. Continue on Washington Street for 2 miles until it intersects with Route 209. Go left and approximately 0.2 mile ahead on the right is the Winnegance store. Once you see the Winnegance store, High Street will continue off to the right, while Route 209 S will veer left. Go right here. Stay on this road, High Street (which turns into Campbells Pond Road), for 2.3 miles. Go right on Birch Point Road. (The Meadowbrook Camping facility will be straight ahead.) After 0.7 mile on Birch Point Road you will see the one-car (nose in) parking space on the right. Pull in as far off the pavement as you can so your dogs can exit your vehicle safely.

Falmouth Community Park Trail (Falmouth)

Honorable Mention

The majority of these trails skirt along the edge of large green athletic fields. During the school year, the fields are in use, and teenagers, adults, and children are present. When the fields are used for sporting events, dogs are not allowed to be off-leash. The trails are connected via bridges, and once past the athletic fields, the trail goes along

the edge of a large hayfield into the woods and along a small brook. The trails total about 3 miles of walking. There are four different parking lots, and you can enter the trail from any of these lots.

Directions: You can take Exit 53 off Interstate 95 and pick up Route 100/26 going north. Immediately go right on Winn Road. The entrance to this park is 0.3 mile up on the right.

Coming from the north, take Exit 11 off Interstate 295, the Falmouth Spur, which connects you to I-95. Once on I-95 go north to Exit 53 and follow the directions above.

Falmouth Nature Preserve (Falmouth)

Overall Score	🐾🐾	Difficulty	🔥🔥
Average Time	45 mins.–1.5 hrs.	Parking	🦴🦴🦴
Average Distance	1–3 miles	Trail Markings	★★★

It clearly states that dogs must be on a leash at this property, but truth be told there are not a lot of people who frequent this park, so use your own judgement. (It was recommended to me as an off-leash dog-walking area!) This is a very dense and dark forest. It seems to be almost 10 degrees cooler in the woods. Because of this denseness the mosquitoes and other insects are horrid in the summer months. Come prepared with bug spray. There is a vast network of trails here, and the only map you will see is the one at the parking area, so study it and get your

bearings. This property is owned by The Nature Conservancy and is 84 acres in size. There are some wet areas, and planks or elevated walkways have been installed in most places. Roots stick up out of the ground, so watch your footing and wear good shoes. Please bring your own poop bags and leave no trace behind. The trails are well marked, and they connect and cross with each other frequently, so you can make several trail choices along the way. If you do meet someone else, put your dogs on a leash and respect the other patrons.

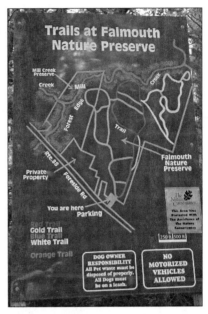

Directions: Route 88 in Falmouth runs north/ south along Casco Bay. This preserve is located between U.S. Route 1 and Route 88. Take Interstate 295 to exit 10. After exiting go south on U.S. Route 1 for 0.3 mile, then turn left onto Depot Road. This road connects with Route 88 (Foreside Road) in less than 0.2 mile. Go north on Route 88 for about 0.4 mile; the preserve entrance is across from 177 Foreside Road (a.k.a. Route 88). It is a gravel drive to your left as you are traveling north on Route 88. Drive in to the parking area and trailhead.

Fort Popham Beach (Popham)

Overall Score	🐾🐾🐾🐾	Difficulty	Beach
Average Time	40 mins.	Parking	🦴🦴🦴
Average Distance	>1–4 miles	Trail Markings	None

Dogs are allowed on this beach all year round. It can afford owners and pets with a salty-sandy-wet adventure. Poop bags are provided near the first set of "outhouses" that you see once you leave your car and walk toward the beach. (The fort will be on your left at this point.) However, the poop-bag station is often empty, so it is a good idea to bring your own. It is expected that you keep your dogs on a leash, especially when the beach is crowded. Many people bring their dogs here, and not all dogs are well socialized. People do let their dogs off-leash as they walk further down the beach and get away from the crowds. Make sure your dogs are on voice command, because many people wander up and down the beach and do not wish to be accosted by wet and sandy four-legged animals. In the off-season you seldom meet many people, and thus more owners let their dogs roam free. Please respect the posted signs, and be sure to clean up after your pet. If your pet usually drinks a lot on outings, bring a portable bowl and fresh water, as the water here is salty, and it will make dogs sick if they drink too much of it!

Directions: Take U.S. Route 1 to Bath. Coming from the south on U.S. Route 1, get off at the second exit in Bath, High Street/Phippsburg, and go right at the top of the ramp. This is High Street, a.k.a. Route 209 S. Stay on Route 209 S for 16.4 miles. If you are coming into Bath from the north, exit U.S. Route 1 in Bath and follow the road under the overpass; you will see signs for Route 209 South. Make a left under the overpass. This puts you onto Washington Street, which intersects with Route 209 S after about 2

miles. From this intersection keep going south on 209 for 14.6 miles. After about 10 miles, Route 209 and 216 will split; make sure you veer left and stay on Route 209 S. After another 3 miles you will pass the entrance to Popham Beach State Park. (In this park dogs are only allowed in the off-season, September 30 to April 1; and you have to pay a fee.) Keep driving past the park entrance until you enter the town of Popham. Go to the end of the road and park near the fort. Keep your dogs leashed until you get well onto the beach and away from the more populated section near the restaurant and store.

Freeport Recreation Facility (Freeport)

Overall Score	🐾	Difficulty	🔥
Average Time	>20 mins.	Parking	🦴🦴🦴
Average Distance	0.4–4 miles	Trail Markings	None

A little for everyone here: a large ball field, swing sets, trails, and open areas to run and play in. The trails start into the woods to the left of the baseball diamond. Just keep walking toward the woods on the left side of the fence around the back of home plate and to the right of the play set. The trails are not marked, but you will end up on the backside of the dump/recycling  facility in Freeport. They are ATV and snowmobile trails that are wide but unmarked. This is a flat walk with many connecting trails, so bring a GPS unit or compass and keep your bearings. There are some mud holes and wet areas, so the mosquitoes are a problem in the summer months. Not all children who come and play on the swing sets like dogs, so please keep control of your pets around the jungle gym if there are others present. I have met people who stop to let their dogs romp and play on the ball field as a

respite from sitting
in the car while the
humans shop and
explore Freeport.
Please bring your own
poop bags and clean
up after your pets.
There is no water
availability here, so it
is a good idea to bring
water and a dish for
your dogs.

Directions: Take Exit 22 off Interstate 295 in Freeport. Go
west off the ramp toward Durham Road. On Durham Road
go left, following the signs to Hedgehog Mountain (and
Bradbury Mountain State Park). Go 1.1 miles on Durham
Road, which changes its name to Pownal Road after a
sharp 90-degree right-hand turn. This recreation area will
be on your left, directly after the left that would take you
into the Freeport Recycling Facility and Hedgehog Mountain. (See the description for Hedgehog Mountain on page
58.) There is a large gravel parking area.

Frog Hollow Farm (South Windham)

Overall Score	🐾	Difficulty	🔥
Average Time	45 mins.–2 hrs.	Parking	Off-street
Average Distance	1–3.5 miles	Trail Markings	None

Although there is no formal parking area, there is some
space in front of the sign for the farm where you can park
(nose in). This is "varied terrain, with pastures grown
up into 50-year-old woodlots, several ravines with small
brooks leading into the north branch of Little River, fields,
two small ponds, and a deer wintering area," according to
the Windham Land Trust website. I had a hard time finding any formal trail through these fields, so the going can
be a bit tough. As you come down the hill from where you

parked, the tall brush hides the fact that there is a great deal of standing water (about 10 to 12 inches), so rubber boots are a good idea. Walk on the rudimentary trail about 0.75 mile from the parking place, and you will get to a brook. There are lots of fallen trees, so the route turns into quite an obstacle course. It is a pretty piece of property, donated by a local resident who owned the land for over 50 years, Mr. J. Dunham. It is there for the use, and the local residents welcomed the dogs with open arms. Because the fields are not mown, beware of the possibility of ticks. Bring your own poop bags and be a responsible dog owner—clean up!

Directions: This place is located northwest of Portland. You can take Exit 48 off Interstate 95 and follow the signs to Route 25 West (you might be on Route 25 Business for a bit), then pick up Route 237 West toward South Windham. You can also come down Route 202 from Gray to the intersection of Routes 202 and 237. Once you get to the intersection of Routes 202 N and 237 W (there is a roundabout here), go west on Route 237 for 1.5 miles. Go left on Winslow Road; 0.6 mile down on the right you will see the "Dunham Frog Hollow Farm" sign. Pull in to the right of it. Do not park on the roadway that continues past the preserve entrance—it serves private homes.

George J. Mitchell Field (South Harpswell)

Overall Score	🐾🐾	Difficulty	🔥
Average Time	45 mins.–1 hr.	Parking	🦴🦴🦴
Average Distance	+1.5 miles	Trail Markings	Stone pillars

A bit of a drive, but a great place for off-leash romping, because the entire place is fenced in and safe. This used to be a Navy base, so the walk itself is flat, easy, and paved. There is a small pond and lots of grassy open field. There are picnic tables set up down by the water. The walking trail starts to the right of the entrance, but if you want to go in the clockwise direction, you will have to start walking straight ahead and then veer to the left. The trail markers are blue cement pillars with small white arrows. The main paved walking road is 1.5 miles long. Because it is paved it is reminiscent of the Brunswick Walking Path, but it has a much larger "free" area for dogs to run and play. You can continue walking on a gravel road that completes a loop and brings you back to where you parked, making the entire route about 2 miles long. There is a wooded area

with a stream that dogs can explore. This is a 116-acre property. On clear days it is possible to see Mt. Washington in the distance. Please bring your own poop bags, and do clean up after your pets.

Note: Because this is such a flat and easy walk, several patrons appeared to be elderly and gentle walkers. If your dogs are rambunctious or jump up on people, please take

control of your animals when you meet other patrons and respect them and their pets.

Directions: Take U.S. Route 1 or Interstate 295 to Brunswick (exit 28). Go into Brunswick and take Maine Street toward Bowdoin College. Turn (left or right, depending on your approach direction) onto Route 123 South (at the intersection of Bath Road and Route 123 near Bowdoin College). Stay on Route 123 S for 11.1 miles; right when you start losing hope of arriving, you will see the blue water tower on the right side of the road. Also on the right is the George Mitchell Field sign; turn in here and park to the left of the driveway, parallel to the fence. Enter by the small brick building.

Greenleaf Preserve (Phippsburg)

Overall Score	🐾🐾	Difficulty	🔥 🔥
Average Time	<1 hr.	Parking	🦴
Average Distance	1.2 miles	Trail Markings	★

This is a small preserve, privately owned but open for public use. There are a few different options for you and your pets: a marked trail that leads down to the Kennebec River or an unmarked single track that leads through the woods (this is an out and back). The mosquitoes are out-of-sight in the summer months, so bring lots of repellent. There are privately owned properties all around the border of this preserve, so be careful to heed the posted signs. The woods are dense, and there are some wet

areas to maneuver around if you choose the unmarked trail. The view at the water's edge is pretty. Please clean up after yourself and your pets.

Directions: Take U.S. Route 1 to Bath. Coming from the south on U.S. Route 1, get off at the second exit in Bath, High Street/Phippsburg, and go right at the top of the ramp. This is High Street, a.k.a. Route 209 South. Stay on Route 209 S for 3.9 miles. If you are coming into Bath from the north, exit U.S. Route 1 in Bath and follow the road under the overpass; you will see signs for Route 209 South. Make a left under the overpass, in front of the Bath post office. This left puts you onto Washington Street, which eventually intersects with Route 209 S (after 2 miles). On route 209 S go left on Fiddlers Reach Road. After 0.3 mile go right on Atwood Lane. Go 0.3 mile on Atwood Lane; the road is dirt and gets rougher as you continue straight ahead. You will be in the woods; veer left and travel down an incline, and you will see the Greenleaf Preserve green and yellow sign on the left. Parking is directly to the left of the preserve's sign. Continue walking along the road; the marked trail down to the water is on the right (red trail blazes on the trees). You can also go left at the preserve sign (into the dense woods on a single-track); this trail is unmarked.

Griggs Preserve (Newcastle)

Overall Score	🐾🐾🐾🐾	Difficulty	🔥🔥🔥
Average Time	1 hr.	Parking	🦴🦴🦴
Average Distance	2 + miles	Trail Markings	★★★

A well-kept, slightly hard-to-find, very peaceful preserve—67 acres of hiking, pretty views, and unique sights. A free map is available at the informational kiosk near the parking area. The map is very accurate, and you can read about the worthy sights on the trail, which are marked by numbers on nearby trees. The trail is well maintained and the tree blazes are clear, but it is narrow, with at times unstable footing, so bring good footwear. There are three main trails, adding up to about 2 miles of hiking. There are some fairly steep inclines and some fast descents, which are curvy and weave through the trees. There are two different areas that afford water views, but no water access can be had, which is a bit of a drawback in the hotter summer months (especially for water-loving dogs). The main trail is the White Shad Trail, marked by a cute white fish on some of the trees. The others are called the Red Salmon Loop and the Blue Heron Leg. Dogs are allowed off-leash here. Please bring your own poop bags and clean up after your pets.

Directions: Take U.S. Route 1 North from Brunswick through Bath, over the bridge past Bath Iron Works to Woolwich. Reset the mile counter on your car as you come across the U.S. Route 1 bridge into Woolwich. Continue north on U.S. Route 1 for a total of 11 (nearly 11.1) miles. Some mile markers are as follows: after 8.6 miles on U.S. Route 1 you will be in Wiscasset; you will continue over a long bridge following signs toward Booth Bay (without actually turning south off U.S. Route 1). Continue on U.S. Route 1 through Edgecomb. At the 11+-mile mark go left on Cochran Road. Continue on Cochran Road for 0.9 mile; it is paved. Go left again on Trails End Road; this road is dirt (it comes in from the left as Cochran Road veers sharply right). It is marked "private drive," but you can drive in to the preserve on it. Parking is on the left on a slightly steep incline.

Hardy Road Trail (Falmouth)

Overall Score	🐾🐾🐾	Difficulty	🔥
Average Time	1–1.5 hrs.	Parking	🦴
Average Distance	1–2.7 miles	Trail Markings	None

This trail is on a Town of Falmouth-owned easement on private land along the Falmouth-Westbrook town line. No motorized vehicles are allowed, so it is a safe and fun place to bring off-leash dogs. The trails are wide, almost like a single-track ATV road, and there is a vast network of such trails. Some places are wet, because you will be walking near wetlands and crossing the Meander Brook. In the winter cross-country skiers seek out this area. One area in particular was so saturated that it acted like a small pond, and the dogs had a great time chasing dragonflies and running through the swampy water. The trails are not marked, so bring a compass or GPS unit. Private

homes and properties are all around, so if you did feel disoriented or lost, you are sure to end up in someone's back yard and you can ask for directional guidance (if need be). Leave only footprints behind.

Directions: From points south of Falmouth, take I-95 North to Exit 53. Off the exit go west on Leighton Road (which changes to Brook Road) for 0.2+ mile. Go right onto Blackstrap Road. After less than 0.5 mile, Blackstrap Road veers to the right, and Hardy Road continues straight. Pick up Hardy Road and go an additional 0.6 mile after this split. The preserve parking is off to the left side of the road; the pavement widens here and allows for parking. You will see a gate, and the trailhead is directly to the right of the gate. Be careful when unloading (and subsequently loading) your pets from your car, since you are so close to the road. Hardy Road is 1.7 miles long, so if you pass the preserve the first time you drive up this road, go to the end and turn around. After turning around the preserve parking will be at the widening of the road 1.1 miles from the end (on the right) as you come down a slight hill.

Harpswell Cliff Trails (Harpswell)

Overall Score	🐾🐾🐾🐾	Difficulty	🔥🔥🔥
Average Time	1–2 hrs.	Parking	✓✓✓
Average Distance	1–4 miles	Trail Markings	★★★

This is a peaceful walk with wonderful views. It has some up and down sections, a few small bridge crossings, as well as dense woods and lots of waterways. Several wild turkeys were spotted and subsequently chased on these trails, so please be alert for this possibility. The trails seem well worn, but I have yet to meet anyone else out here. There is an area with Fairy Cabins, which I will allow you to read about on your own at the trailhead. This trail system is well worth multiple visits. The trail rules dictate that you must pick up after your pets, but they do not need to be on a leash. There are no free maps, but maps are stapled to

certain trees at some of the trail intersections. Follow white blazes for the 2.25-mile trail or the yellow blazes for the 1.75-mile loop. The trails are well kept, and the markings are clear and easy to follow. The yellow and white trails do overlap. The overlook at the top of the cliff is fabulous, but be careful—it is a 150-foot drop straight down. You can look across the cove and see people (if there are any) on the Long Reach Trail (see the description and directions for this walk on page 66).

Directions: Take U.S. Route 1 between Brunswick and Bath to the Cooks Corner exit. Once you come off the exit, go straight through the large intersection; you are now on Route 24 South. You will be following the signs to Bailey's Island, Orr's Island, and Cundy's Harbor. (FYI: Route 24 S starts out as Gurnet Road on your car's GPS system.) Stay on Route 24 S for 8.5 miles. You will turn right onto Mountain Road. Look for and follow the signs for Black Sheep Wine Shop. Stay on Mountain Road 1.3 miles. (The winery is 0.7 mile further down this road, so if you want to go there, keep driving.) The Harpswell Town Offices building will be on your right. Turn into the parking lot and stay to the left, driving around to the back of the building.

Parking and the trailhead are in the leftmost corner of the parking lot. Bring your own poop bags, it is also a good idea to bring some clean water for you and your pets on this walk. Water access is fairly limited.

Hawkes-Tow Path Land Trust (Gorham/Windham)

Honorable Mention

A bit hard to find and parking is virtually nonexistent, but this area has possibilities. The property is owned by Presumpscot Regional Land Trust (formerly Gorham-Sebago Regional Land Trust). There is over 2000 feet of Presumpscot River frontage and 41 acres for public use. This land trust is located near the remains of the Oxford and Cumberland Canal. The trail is wide and easy to follow. You can take this trail from the Tow Path Road area along the river all the way up to Gambo Road.

Directions: To get to Tow Path Road (in South Windham, north of Gorham), you must get on Route 202/4 North out of Gorham. You can get on this road by taking Exit 47 (or Exit 48) off Interstate 95 and traveling on Route 25 West to Route 202/4 North. Or you can come south on Route 202/4 from Gray (approximately 11.5 miles from Gray). After four miles north of Gorham on Route 202/4 N, Tow Path Road comes in on your left after you have gone through the intersection of Routes 237 and 202  (immediately after Hudson Road). Go left and travel 0.2 mile to the end of the road. The trail starts dead ahead. You will have to ask permission to park on the left shoulder in the last house's yard. Leave a note on your windshield if no one is home: "Hiking."

Hedgehog Mountain (Freeport)

Overall Score	🐾🐾🐾	Difficulty	🔥🔥
Average Time	1–1.5 hrs.	Parking	🦴🦴
Average Distance	1–2.7 miles	Trail Markings	★★★

You will frequently meet others with their dogs off-leash here. It is a fun little jaunt up a hill and down the other side. If you try really hard you may get a glimpse of snow-covered Mount Washington from the top of Hedgehog Mountain. This area is often utilized, well marked and kept up nicely. There is no map, but the light blue trail markings on the trees are easy to spot and easy to follow. The terrain is varied. The woods are dense, so please be careful (especially in the fall) if the leaves on the ground are wet, because they get slippery. It is not a very wet area, but expect mosquitoes and other bugs in the summer months. Dogs are assumed to be on "voice command." There are signs right at the parking area asking pet owners to please clean up after their pets. Poop bags and a separate "animal waste" receptacle are available, so please utilize them. Not only can you go to the top of Hedgehog Mountain, but there are also the Wentworth and Stonewall trails to explore. There is little or no water here, so if it is hot bring fluids for you and your pets. Open all year. Please be safe and equip yourself and your dogs with blaze orange colors in hunting season (approx. late Oct through mid-Dec).

Directions: Take I-295 north or south to Exit 22, Freeport/ Durham. Go west at the top of the ramp and continue to the intersection with Durham Road (it's a T); go left here. Stay on Durham Road exactly 1.1 miles. Durham Road makes a sharp 90-degree turn to the right and changes it's name to Pownal Road. After 1.1 miles you will see a yellow sign on the right that states "Recycling Facility Entrance 500 feet." This is your cue to slow down; you will be making a sharp left onto Land Fill Road (as if you really are going to the landfill). Stay on Land Fill Road for 0.2 mile, and you will see the parking area on the left. The road to the landfill continues straight; if the landfill is closed, there is a locked gate.

Higgins Mountain Preserve (Georgetown)

Overall Score	🐾🐾	Difficulty	🔥 🔥
Average Time	15–20 mins.	Parking	🦴
Average Distance	0.68 miles	Trail Markings	★★

This is a Lower Kennebec Regional Land Trust (LKRKT), a rocky, hilly climb; straight up and then straight back down again to the car. All told, this loop is only 0.68 mile in

length, and you'll be back at the car in about 20 minutes. But it certainly is pretty at the top. If any of your canine friends are geriatric or limited in movement at all, this may not be the walk for you. It is a rocky scramble to the top and a gentler but still rocky walk back down to the car (if you go in the clockwise direction, i.e. left from the parking lot). Going in the counterclockwise direction, the ascent is less severe, and you will start out in the woods. Either way you go, you will encounter rocky ledges, stone crevices, and dramatic rocks that must be maneuvered around. Since there are not many trees along the trail, you will be following small "towers" or "piles" of rocks. This walk may not be the most fun for your four-legged friends, but it can be a good, quick workout. Please be careful of your own and your pets' footing. You will hear the traffic from Route 127 at all times while on this walk, because you are parallel to the road. The top offers good views and places to sit on the rocks and rest. Please bring your own poop bags and pick up after yourself and your dogs.

Directions: Take U.S. Route 1 from Brunswick north through Bath and continue over the bridge to Woolwich. In Woolwich bear right, going south on Route 127 (toward Georgetown). If you are coming from the north, head south on U.S. Route 1 and take the right-hand exit (right before the bridge over the Kennebec River to Bath) in order to catch Route 127 South—watch for signs for Reid State Park. Stay on Route 127 S for 7.8 miles. This road winds and bends in and out of tree-covered sections, past homes, and at 4.7 miles you will cross over a narrow bridge. At exactly 7.8 miles the road gets wider, and on the right shoulder an outcropping makes a small parking area. The sign for Higgins Mountain Preserve is on the right, off the pavement by about 15 feet. Park here on the sandy shoulder and catch the trail either starting out to the left or the right of the informational kiosk. No maps are available for visitors. Since parking is along the very busy Route 127, be careful when letting your dogs in or out of the car so they do not run into traffic.

Hinckley Park (South Portland)

Overall Score	🐾🐾🐾	Difficulty	🔥
Average Time	>30 mins.	Parking	🦴🦴🦴
Average Distance	1–3 miles	Trail Markings	None

This is a large 40-acre park with lots of trails, small ponds, bridges and plenty to smell. A real gem in the middle of a populated area. Although a bit hard to find, this place promises lots of fun. Many people come here with dogs, and most are off-leash. This place is also open in the wintertime. The walking trails are wide and well worn. The terrain is fairly flat with a few rolling hills. The trails run into the woods, along the ponds, and over some bridges. There is a large paved parking area. A poop-bag dispenser is located at the trailhead. Please clean up after your pets and dispose of the excrement in the appropriate receptacles.

Directions: From Interstate 295 in South Portland take the U.S. Route 1 exit and go south on Route 1. You will quickly come to the intersection of Route 1 and Broadway. Go left on Broadway (toward Portland's waterway). Stay on Broadway until it intersects with Ocean Avenue (also called

Route 77). Go right on Ocean Avenue, heading south.
Then go immediately right onto Highland Avenue. Hinckley Park is on the left before you get to Stillman Street, less
than a mile away.

Hyde School Forest (Bath)

Overall Score	🐾🐾	Difficulty	🔥🔥
Average Time	45 mins.–1.5 hrs.	Parking	🦴🦴
Average Distance	0.7–3 miles	Trail Markings	None

This is a good place to go if you don't want to see anyone yet feel the need to go out among the trees. These
are mostly ATV single tracks, along with some trails that
belong to the private high school in Bath, Hyde School.
This is rolling terrain, mostly out and back trails that take
you down to a freshwater lake (good swimming for dogs).
There aren't any trail markers per se, but little signs posted
on various trees with the symbol of an ATV or snowmobile let you know you are on the "right" trail. You can take
one set of trails (from your car, enter the woods and head
to your right), which leads back to Bath Road. Another
trail goes from your vehicle, straight across the athletic
field, into the woods and then continues straight; you
will end up at the aforementioned lake. If you go to the
left, just before entering the woods you will loop around

toward the back of Hyde School and eventually back on High Street. It is a must that you bring a GPS unit or compass to this property. Right where you park you will see signs that state "Pets are welcome on a leash," this refers to the track and the athletic field near the parking area, especially if students are using the field. Bring your own poop bags and clean up after your pets.

Directions: The easiest way to get here is by going to the Bath Holiday Inn's parking lot—the hotel can easily be seen from U.S. Route 1 (coming north into Bath). However, coming into Bath from the north is a bit different; you must go over the bridge across the Kennebec River on U.S. Route 1 S and exit just past the shopping center and McDonalds (visible on your right); this is the Congress Avenue exit. Go left onto Congress Avenue at the bottom of the ramp. Congress Avenue Ts with Bath Road; go left again and then right on Richardson Street. (You are essentially getting back onto the on-ramp for U.S. Route 1 N when Richardson Street comes in on your right.) Directly across the parking lot of the Holiday Inn is Richardson Street, and directly across Richardson Street is Redlon Street. Stay on Redlon Street until it ends—veer slightly to the right when the road forks. You will see the parking area on the right—an athletic field is to your left and a track is on the far right. You will start walking directly through the red brick gates, across a large mown field (old football field) and into the woods to the trails.

Jamies Pond Wildlife Management Area (Hallowell)

Overall Score	🐾🐾🐾🐾	Difficulty	🔥🔥
Average Time	1–4 hrs.	Parking	🦴🦴🦴
Average Distance	>2 miles	Trail Markings	★★★

A very well-marked trail system that primarily follows the
north side of the Jamies Pond. The State of Maine Wildlife
Management Area website says this about the property:
"There are a total of 840 acres here that touch the periph-
ery of three communities: Hallowell, Manchester, and
Farmingdale. The pond is 75 feet deep and 107 acres wide,
and it is stocked with brook trout and splake, while naturally also containing bass and pickerel." There are locator
maps at each trailhead and trail intersection, but there are
no maps available for the taking. The Pond Trail has two
separate loops, both of which give hikers a nice view of
Jamies Pond. The Vernal
Pool Trail goes over a slight
ridge and includes large
glacial erratic boulders and
huge pine trees. The Forest
Trail is the biggest loop;
it passes through dense
woods and wetlands and
runs along a stream, all on
the north side of Jamies
Pond. All the trails inter-

connect and allow hikers to choose how long or short a
hike they want to take. Please bring your own poop bags
and clean up after your dogs. If you plan to hike far, bring
a snack for your dogs. A compass or GPS unit might be a
good idea to take along. This property is well worth multiple visits. Don't miss the fall leaf color around the lakes.

Directions: From Hallowell (just south of Augusta) take
Outlet Road to Jamies Pond Road, which is dirt. Fork-
ing off to the right, there is a small street sign indicating
Jamies Pond Road. Take the dirt road 0.3 mile and look
for the turnoff to the pond on your left. You can also park
along Jamies Pond Road (easier in the winter), but make
sure you are off the roadway completely. Jamies Pond Road
is also called Meadow Hill Road on some GPS systems, so
be careful. From Manchester there is access to this area
from both Collins Road and Meadow Hill Road. Collins
Road is a right-hand turn off Pond Road (which runs north

along the Cobbosseecontee Lake). If you are coming south on Pond Road, go left on Meadow Hill Road and you will see the parking for Jamies Pond Wildlife Management Area on the right side of the road before it turns to dirt and becomes Jamies Pond Road.

Little River Property (Gorham)

Honorable Mention

There are over 2 miles of trails here, maintained by Presumpscot Regional Land Trust (formerly Gorham-Sebago Land Trust). This property encompasses 28 acres and offers trails and scenery through woodlands and along the Little River. This is fairly flat terrain, and in places the trails can become a bit overgrown in late summer. There is an informational kiosk but no maps are available for the taking, so you may need to memorize the map posted at the parking area. Dogs are allowed here, but please bring your own poop bags and clean up after your pets. According to the trust's web site, "it holds a conservation easement of woodland bordering the river, protecting its scenic value and wildlife habitat and giving opportunity for neighbors to enjoy nature's beauty."

Directions: To get here, you will have to get onto Route 202/4 North out of Gorham. You can get on this road by taking Exit 47 (or Exit 48) off I-95 and traveling on Route 25 West (or Route 25 business) for about 1.6 miles to

Route 202/4 North. Or you can come south on Route 202/4 from Gray (approximately 12.5 miles southeast of Gray). This preserve is directly west of Route 202 off the roadway, so you may see it and go on by, only to turn around and go back. It is located just about 2 miles north of Gorham on Route 202 N. The parking area is small and gravel. You can see the informational kiosk from Route 202/4.

Long Reach Preserve (Harpswell)

Overall Score	🐾🐾🐾	Difficulty	🔥🔥🔥
Average Time	1 hr.	Parking	🦴🦴🦴
Average Distance	1.1 miles	Trail Markings	★★★

A fabulous combination of up-and-down hikes, water views, woods, and trees at this very neat Harpswell Heritage Land Trust (HHLT) property. The trails are well marked, although at times the white paint on the trees is spaced out so much that you may have to "search" a bit for the next marker—looking back the way you came is always helpful. It is by no means a wide trail, but it is reasonably easy to find your way through the trees. There is a free map, which is quite accurate, and it points out places where the view of Quahog Bay is worth a Kodak® moment. There is limited shore access into Long Reach Cove. In addition to the "marked" trail, the map indicates

an "unmarked" loop that runs between the marked trail, the cove, and Route 24, so keep that in mind if you feel adventurous. This preserve offers 93 acres of space to explore. Although the marked trail only measures about 1+ mile in length, it does take a solid hour to get around the loop. At the southernmost point of the trail, when you are on the shore of Long Reach Cove, you are actually directly across from the Cliff Trail, which starts behind the Harpswell Town Offices. Perhaps if you started out on this trail and a friend started out on the other, you would reach the cove simultaneously and be able to wave to each other! Please bring your own poop bags and pick up after your dogs.

Note: In the summer of 2008 signs were posted at the parking area that stated that this is a day-use park only and dogs have to be leashed. The trail map still states that dogs can be on voice command. Make your own judgment call here.

Directions: Take U.S. Route 1 (north out of Brunswick or south from Bath) to the Cooks Corner exit and head south (straight through the large four-way intersection) on Route 24. Stay on Route 24 S for 6.9 miles. On your right you will see the Trufant-Summerton ball field. Pull into the ball field's parking area and stay to the right. Way up on a tree you will see the Long Reach Preserve sign pointing to the right; park as far off to the right (on the gravel) as you can. The trailhead starts here; you will spot the informational kiosk. Maps are available. You can take the loop in the clockwise or counterclockwise direction.

Lovers Lane (Topsham)

Overall Score	🐾🐾	Difficulty	🔥🔥
Average Time	30 mins.–1 hr.	Parking	Off-street
Average Distance	1–3 miles	Trail Markings	None

A little-known ATV and snowmobile area, well worth a visit. There is a myriad of well-used trails here that appear to be utilized primarily by people on motorized vehicles. This is not a preserve, so no official map or trail markings

exist, but there are frequent signs related to the use of these roads by ATVs or snowmobiles. These trails are open all year. You may want to bring a compass or GPS unit. One trail has houses along one side, so you will be walking and gazing into people's backyards. This place gets very muddy after rainfall or in the spring when snow is melting. On the weekends watch out for those motorized vehicles; they can come up on you and your pets pretty quickly.

Directions: Take the Topsham/Route 196/24 exit if you are coming from points north on U.S. Route 1. Go north to the first lighted intersection—this is Route 196 intersecting with Route 24. Go right here and then take the immediate next left; this is Middlesex Road, a.k.a. Route 24 N. Alternately, if you are coming north on Interstate 295, take Exit 31. This is the Topsham/Route 196 exit. Go south on Route 196 toward U.S. Route 1. As you come down a long hill toward the on-ramps for U.S. Route 1 North and South, take a left toward Richmond and Route 24. Then take the very next left onto Route 24 N (Middlesex Road). Go 1 mile on Route 24 N, and Lovers Lane will come in from the right; it is a dirt road. Go right onto Lovers Lane. After 0.1 mile the first ATV/snowmobile trail comes in from your right, but this is not a good place to park so keep going. Go an additional 0.2 mile on Lovers Lane; the road turns sharply right, and you can park off to the left here, ATV trails and a field are visible on your left side. You can also continue going right on Lovers Lane and then immediately taking the left onto Eider Lane. Take Eider Lane to the end, where after 0.5 mile it Ts with Hunter Lane. Go left onto Hunter Lane and park off the roadway where the trails start (directly in front of you). Go either left or right on the ATV tracks from here.

Lowell Preserve (Windham)

Overall Score	🐾🐾🐾	Difficulty	🔥🔥🔥
Average Time	1–4 hrs.	Parking	🦴🦴🦴
Average Distance	1–8 miles	Trail Markings	★

What a vast expanse of area to take your off-leash pooches! There are 308 lovely acres here at your disposal. The trail starts out up a small incline on a lovely wood-chipped path. Then you go into the woods and work your way toward Little Duck Pond along the McIntosh Brook. There are some wet spots here, and the footing is at times slick, so wear good shoes. There are no trail maps or tree markers on the trail, so it is wise to bring a compass or GPS unit. You will be following vehicular signs that pertain to ATVs and snowmobiles. Since ATVs, snowmobiles, hunting, and fishing are all permitted here, please take the appropriate precautions with respect to your pets and your own safety. Wear blaze orange in the fall; and be aware that people on motorized vehicles can come up on you or your animals quickly. You will return to your vehicle the same way you entered the preserve. Above all, have a lovely time.

Directions: Take Interstate 295 South (if you are coming from Bath/ Brunswick/ Freeport or points further north or east) to Exit 11 (the Falmouth Connector to Interstate 95).  Go south on I-95 to exit 48. Coming from the south, go north on I-95 to exit 48. This is the Route 25/302 – Riverside Street exit. Go north on Riverside Street for a little more than 1 mile—you will be traveling through a business-park area. Go left on Route 302 West. Stay on Route 302 W for 5.9 (nearly 6) miles. Go right on Albion Road and travel 1.5 miles. Go right again, this time onto Falmouth Road, traveling west. After 0.5 mile on Falmouth Road you will see the signs for a fire station on the left; pull into this parking area. Park in front of the fire station and pick up the trailhead to the left of the building. There is a small play area and baseball field to the right of the paved parking area if you stand with your back to Falmouth Road.

Maine Mountain Division Trail (Windham/Gorham/Standish)

Honorable Mention

This is a long trail that has been created parallel to old railroad tracks running between the towns of Windham, Gorham, and Standish. All told, it is in excess of 4 miles long in one direction. The surface is hard-packed gravel and in some places wood or cement. I wouldn't say it is ideal for off-leash dogs, but you are permitted to have dogs here. There are some nice athletic fields near the Windham parking area of this trail, so perhaps you can play fetch or let your pets romp around there for a bit. Please bring leashes in case other patrons who are using the trail do not wish to be accosted. Horseback riding and biking are permitted, so be alert. Be sure to bring your own poop bags and clean up after your pets.

Directions: This trail has several access points. To reach the access point in South Windham, get on Route 202/4 North. You can get on this road by taking Exit 47 off Interstate 95 and traveling on Route 25 to Route 237 West, which leads you to Route 202 N. Or you can come south on Route 202/4 from Gray. Gambo Road is west of Route 202/4, approximately 3.5 miles south on Route 202/4 from the intersection of Route 302, Route 202, and Route 4 (a large roundabout called Fosters Corner) in Windham Center. Once you turn onto Gambo Road, go 0.3 mile and make a right into the parking area (a long dirt driveway). There is an informational kiosk here, and you can see the athletic fields beyond the gate on the left side. If you continue on Gambo Road you will come to a lovely covered bridge.

Maine Public Reserve Land (Gray)

Honorable Mention

This is public-use land and no hunting is allowed here, so it is a good place to take your canines; there is a possibility that you could be chased by cows if it is summer or early fall. There are single-track dirt trails, a gravel road, areas of overgrown path, and sand dunes. Lots of variety

here, plenty of things to see and smell, and lots of space. But there are no trail markers or informational kiosk, so you'll need to bring a compass or a GPS unit. You will be exploring an area that is between a busy road, railroad tracks, and the Royal River, so you probably won't get too lost (ha! famous last words). If you do happen into the field where the cows live, just turn around and go back out. You would have to cross the railroad tracks in order to allow your dogs to take a dip in the river, so I don't recommend that. (I never recommend or trust the idea of walking on or near railroad tracks.) This place isn't for people who like marked trails, specific loops, or the organization often present at land trusts; out here you are on your own.

Directions: From Portland or points south, take either Interstate 95 or Routes 26/100 North to Gray (Exit 63 off I-95). Go north on Route 4/100/202 for 3 miles. Go right on Morse Road; 2 miles up on your right the road widens and a gravel/dirt area is off to the side. Off into the woods you will see a gravel road with a gate across it; park here and walk up this road. From Yarmouth take Route 115 West to Route 231 North. At the Pineland Estate intersection (Route 231 intersects with Allen Road, Morse Road, and Depot Road), go left on Morse Road. Travel 0.5 mile up Morse Road; the road widens, and a gravel parking area is on the left. Pull into the parking lot and walk up the gravel road past the gate and into the woods. Make sure you unload and load your pets safely.

Marsh River Bog Preserve (Newcastle)

Overall Score	🐾	Difficulty	🔥
Average Time	30–45 mins.	Parking	🦴🦴
Average Distance	1.4 miles	Trail Markings	★★

This property is owned by the Damariscotta River Association. It encompasses 54 acres of river, bog, two different trails, and power lines. The deer ticks and horseflies enjoy this area in the summer, so be ready to bathe in bug spray. Please spray your pets, too. There are some neat man-made bridges; good trail markings, and lots of tall marsh grass to gallop through. There are a couple of white trails that make small loops or out-and-backs from the main blue trail. A trail goes out to the "bog island" in the middle of the marsh. Taking all the various trail combinations will only add up to a little over a mile in walking distance. This is fairly flat terrain. Please keep your pets under voice command and bring your own poop bags to clean up after them.

Directions: Taking U.S. Route 1 North from Brunswick through Bath, go over the bridge past Bath Iron Works to Woolwich. Reset your mile counter on your car as you come across the U.S. Route 1 bridge into Woolwich. Continue north on U.S. Route 1 for a total of 15.1 (nearly 15.2) miles. Some mile markers are as follows: After 8.6 miles on U.S. Route 1 you will be in Wiscasset; you will

continue over a long bridge following signs toward Booth
Bay (without actually going south on Route 27 to Boothbay). Continue on U.S. Route 1 through Edgecomb. The
sign for the Marsh River Bog Preserve is on the left side of
the road as you approach Newcastle from the south. Park
where the parking sign indicates and take a good look at
the wooden map nailed to a tree as you enter the trailhead. There are no free maps, so get your bearings. The
trails all lead back to the parking area. Please respect all
posted private-property signs.

Marsh River Preserve (Newcastle)

Overall Score	🐾🐾	Difficulty	🔥🔥
Average Time	45 mins.	Parking	🦴🦴
Average Distance	1.25 miles	Trail Markings	★★★

This property has a great deal of Marsh River frontage and
Sherman Marsh views, because half the land runs along
these bodies of water. The Marsh River is in places 100 feet
wide, and it is affected by the tides, so it will swell and
then subside. The parking area is at the end of the road;
it makes a circular drive near the preserve informational

kiosk (almost like a cul-de-sac). The trail is hard-packed dirt, and it goes downhill for a way as you start out from the parking area (down toward the river). The trail blazes and markings are clear and easy to see. There is a free map, and an interpretive trail is built in. Trail intersections are marked by capital letters nailed onto the trees. According to the interpretive map, you will travel 100 feet (in elevation change) as you descend to the river, which you then have to walk back up on the way back (if you go clockwise and follow the interpretive trail in order of the numbers along the trail). Dogs are allowed off-leash as long as they are under voice control of their owners. Please bring your own poop bags and clean up after your pets. Mosquitoes are rampant here since there is so much water, so in the summer months bug spray is a must. This property is owned and maintained by the Sheepscot Valley Conservation Association (SVCA).

Directions: Take U.S. Route 1 North from Brunswick (off Exit 28 on Interstate 295 N/S) through Bath, over the bridge across the Kennebec River (past Bath Iron Works) and into Woolwich. Reset the mile counter on your car as you come across the bridge and travel on U.S. Route 1 for a total of 12.5 miles. Some mile markers are as follows: After 8.6 miles on U.S. Route 1 you will be in Wiscasset; you will continue over a long bridge following signs toward Booth Bay (without actually going south on Route 27 to Boothbay). Continue on through Edgecomb. Once you see the sign for the Sherman Lake rest area, Osprey Point Road, a dirt road, will come in from the left. Go left on Osprey Point Road. Veer left past some mailboxes. You will see a sign for the SVCA with an arrow to the left. Keep going 0.2 mile and you will see the informational kiosk on the left.

Mary's Woods Preserve (Winnegance/North Phippsburg)

Honorable Mention

A lovely but small Phippsburg land preserve; there is only private access and an out-and-back trail in lovely deep and dense woods. The trail goes down toward a wetlands/ swamp area, with a view toward Drummore Bay (although you cannot really see the water). The round trip will probably not take longer than 20 minutes. Please respect people who may be in residence here. Remember, you are "visiting" on privately owned land that is open to visitors only through the kindness of the owners. Bring your own poop bags and leave no trace behind.

Directions: Take U.S. Route 1 to Bath. Coming from the south on U.S. Route 1, get off at the second exit in Bath, High Street/Phippsburg, and go right at the top of the ramp. This is High Street, a.k.a. Route 209 South. Stay on Route 209 S for 3.9 miles. If you are coming into Bath from the north, exit U.S. Route 1 in Bath and follow the road under the overpass; you will see signs for Route 209 South. Make a left under the overpass, in front of the Bath post office. This left is onto Washington Street, which eventually intersects with Route 209 S (2.0 miles). Once Washington Street intersects with Route 209 S travel 2.1 miles. Go left on Fiddlers Reach Road. Almost immediately go right onto Old Ferry Road. Immediately go right again down a driveway that has the number 9 posted on a tree (to your right). This is the driveway for Mary's Woods. The driveway is 0.1 miles long and ends at a small cottage. This is where you will park. The trailhead is marked with a sign on a tree to the left of the house.

Massabesic Experimental Forest–Cooks Brook Management Area (Lyman)

Overall Score	🐾🐾🐾	Difficulty	🔥
Average Time	1–2.5 hrs.	Parking	🦴
Average Distance	1–6 miles	Trail Markings	★

The Massabesic Experimental Forest is owned and operated by the USDA Forest Service. It consists of 3600 acres in both Alfred and Lyman (York County). The one I recommend for walking dogs off-leash, is the Northern Unit near Lyman. This plot is over 1 mile wide and 3+ miles long. A nice gravel road runs through the middle of the property, and ends at Roberts Pond. About 0.3 mile from where you will be entering the forest, the Cooks Brook Trail has an information kiosk (on your left as you walk away from your vehicle) where you can pick up the free trail description leaflet. There are 15 items that are noteworthy along the trail. This is a densely wooded area, so bring your bug spray in the summer months. There are some trail markers in the form of ATV or snowmobile signs (as these types of vehicles are permitted in some parts of these woods), but no formal trail markings exist, so bring a compass or GPS unit.

Directions: This property is very close to the intersection of Route 202, which goes from Hollis to Waterboro/Alfred, and Route 5, which runs from Saco to North Waterboro. From the south, on Interstate 95, take Exit 32 (Route 111), and go west on Route 111 to Route 35 (approximately 5.5 miles). Take a right on Route 35 and go north 5 miles to Route 5. Take a left on Route 5 and continue another 3.3 miles. The gate and entrance to this preserve is on the left side of the road. Park to the right side of the gate; do not block the entrance.

Coming from the north take Exit 36, Interstate 195 (a spur off I-95). Now take Exit 1 off I-195 and go left at the end of the ramp. Proceed 0.5 mile to Route 112 North. Go right on Route 112, and proceed 2.4 miles. Take a left on Loudon Road—there is a white horse fence on the corner. Proceed 1.5 miles on Loudon Road to Route 5 (there is no sign). Take a right on Route 5 and proceed about 7.4 miles—look left. The entrance to this property is on your left. Park to the right side of the gate; do not block the entrance. Be careful when unloading (and later loading) your dogs, since you are close to a busy road.

Merrymeeting Bay Wildlife Management Area (Bowdoinham)

Overall Score	🐾🐾🐾	Difficulty	🔥
Average Time	1+ hrs.	Parking	🦴🦴
Average Distance	1–3 miles	Trail Markings	None

Finding this hidden gem is worth the effort. There are lots of things to chase here and hunting is permitted, so please wear blaze orange in the fall. Some trails go underneath very large power lines. Be aware of your dog's behavior in relation to passing under power lines. Some dogs are greatly

affected by "electrically charged" air, so if your pet tucks his/her tail and starts shaking, please return to your car and leave. You will see the dog's reaction immediately upon entering into the area near or under the power lines. The trails are not marked, but they are wide and easy to follow. In the winter the roads become snowmobile trails. There are lots of wetlands, and the land goes all the way down to Bean Point and Merrymeeting Bay. Please take out what you bring in with you. Keep an eye on your pets if they tend to chase game, as there is an abundance of wildlife here. It may be a good idea to have a GPS unit or compass with you at this location. This is an out-and-back walk.

Directions: Take Route 201 North out of Topsham. Go 1.3 miles to the intersection of Route 201 and Route 196, go straight on Route 201 N for 5.6 miles. Route 138 North will come in from the right. Go right and stay on Route 138 N for 2.9 miles. You are now at the intersection of Route 24 and Route 138 in midtown Bowdoinham. Go left on Route 24 N (also called River Road) for 0.6 mile and then go right on Browns Point Road. Stay on Browns Point Road for 0.9 mile, then go right on Wildes Road; the preserve is at the end of Wildes Road, approximately. 0.8 mile down. Parking is a bit scarce—it is easier to find places not to park. But if you continue down the single track past the brown State of Maine sign, you will come to a plentiful parking lot. There is a gate across the single-track dirt road; park here and start walking.

Merrymeeting Fields Preserve
(Chops Point/North Woolwich)

Overall Score	🐾🐾🐾	Difficulty	🔥
Average Time	1+ hr.	Parking	🦴🦴
Average Distance	1.35 miles	Trail Markings	★★★

This is a Lower Kennebec Regional Land Trust (LKRLT) preserve, which encompasses 125 acres. It has two large fields and two completely separate trail loops, which both start from the lower field. Pick up a map at the parking area to get your bearings. The map is not to scale, but it does illustrate the shape of the preserve and the trail locations. The largest field goes all the way down to Merrymeeting Bay and offers spectacular panoramic picture opportunities. The yellow trail goes off to the north and into the woods. The yellow trail is very flat; it makes a half-moon-shaped circuit and ends up back in the upper field. The blue loop has more uneven terrain (and wild turkeys); it heads in the southern direction from the lower field and ends on Chopps Point Road about 100 yards from the parking area. Look to your left and you should be able to see your vehicle as you exit the blue trail. The dogs can swim in Merrymeeting Bay—be careful (!), the rocks are slippery. There are

small bridges (man-made) that help you and your pooches over the wetter areas on both trails. Please clean up after your pets by bringing your own poop bags.

Note: In the summertime the unmown fields at this location seem to have an inordinate amount of ticks, so please check your dogs closely.

Directions: Take U.S. Route 1 North to Woolwich (over the bridge from Bath). As you come down the hill toward the Subaru dealer on your left (0.3 mile after the end of the bridge), look carefully for signs indicating the turn (to the left) for Route 127 North. If you are coming from the north, drive into Woolwich past the Subaru dealer (on your right) and the Cumberland Farms gas station and then turn right onto Route 127 North. Stay on Route 127 N for 1.7 miles. The turn for Route 128 North comes up fast on your left. Stay on Route 128 N for 4.6 (almost 4.7) miles. Go (sharply) left onto Chopps Point Road at the sign for the Chop Point Church and School. The road turns to dirt almost immediately. Go 0.7 mile and you will see the sign and parking area for the Merrymeeting Fields Preserve on your right. This parking area is not plowed in the winter.

Mid-Coast Hospital Nature Trails (Brunswick/Cooks Corner)

Overall Score	🐾	Difficulty	🔥
Average Time	20–30 mins.	Parking	🦴🦴
Average Distance	0.7 miles	Trail Markings	None

This is a nice surprise in the midst of a dense business area along Bath Road near the local hospital. The trails are very flat and easy to follow, mostly with bark and pine-needle footing. You rarely lose sight of the hospital along this walk, and some of the path even skirts around the parking lot and an outdoor patio behind the big brick hospital building. Dogs are permitted here as long as you pick up their excrement. The trail winds and bends and makes

the most of the wooded area around the hospital. There are no maps or informational kiosk. The trail can be picked up in four different locations, so you have plenty of options as to where to park and start walking. This would be a good place to take elderly, infirm, or smaller dogs. People who like flat, easy walks will like this one too. At least you get out into nature and exercise yourself and your pets. Patients might use this walk for recreation or rehab, so please respect other patrons.

Directions: Because this trail is located by one of the larger hospitals in the Bath/Brunswick area, you can find directions to Mid-Coast Hospital in many places. There are also signs along Bath Road indicating the way to the hospital. Take Interstate 295 either north from Portland or south from Augusta and then take Exit 28 to "Brunswick and U.S. Route 1". Take U.S. Route 1 North and exit at Cooks Corner (there are also signs to Orr's and Bailey Islands here) and go left onto Bath Road at the first large intersection off the exit ramp. Travel on Bath Road for approximately 0.7 to 0.8 mile and the turn into the hospital is on the right (at the blue-and-white H sign). From this turn, one good place to catch the trail is 0.7 mile down Hospital Road on the right hand outer edge of the parking lot. You can also park on the left, behind the Medical Office Building, and start the walk from that end. On the hospital's website you can get a trail map and trail description: www.midcoasthealth.com. There are no formal trailheads or signs, so you have to drive slowly and look into the woods to discover where the trailhead is located.

Miller Park—Paper Mill Trail (Lisbon)

Honorable Mention

Dogs are permitted here, but must be on a leash. The trail is paved and runs along the old Paper Mill Road. The rivers that can be seen from the trail are the Androscoggin and Sabattus. A map is available at the information kiosk; it points out birds and trees that may be of interest. Poop bags are available at the trailhead. The parking area is large and paved. The trail is 0.8 mile long and is an out-and-back adventure. If you wish to walk further, you can continue on the Ricker Farm Trail, which begins at the end of the Paper Mill Trail. This trail is also paved and runs along Mill Street and Upland Road (starting near Lisbon Community School on Mill Street).

Directions: If you are coming from the north, take Interstate 95 to Exit 80 and travel east on Route 196 to Lisbon. The park will be on the left side of the road as you are coming east before you enter downtown Lisbon. You briefly turn onto Frost Hill Road, and the parking area and information kiosk are on the left. If you are coming from Topsham, Bath, or Brunswick, take Route 196 West out of Topsham. Stay on Route 196 W approximately 7.8 miles from the intersection of Route 201 and Route 196 in Topsham. You will go through Lisbon Falls and Lisbon. The park comes up quickly on the right side of Route 196. Turn briefly right onto Frost Hill Road, and the parking area and information kiosk will be on the left.

Montsweag Preserve
(Eastern Woolwich/Montsweag)

Overall Score	🐾🐾🐾	Difficulty	🔥 🔥
Average Time	1 hr.	Parking	Off-street
Average Distance	1.4 miles	Trail Markings	★★

This is a Nature Conservancy property heading down
to the Sheepscot River. It is easier to go in the clockwise
direction, following the royal blue trail markers to your left
first; then the markers will change to a lighter blue-green
color at the end of the loop. Always keep your eye on the
next marker ahead; it isn't always easy to see them. This is
rolling terrain, and the footing is a bit slick as you traverse
and parallel the water along the eastern part of this walk.
There are deer in these woods, so if your dogs are the sort
who chase deer, be aware. The preserve is enclosed on both
sides by private properties with homes, as well as the water
on the third side and the road where you parked on the
fourth. You can take an unmarked trail (which is an extension of the marked trail; it goes straight where the marked
trail goes right) to the point and see the lovely view of the
water, a small island, and the opposite shore. Entry into
the water is possible, but the rocks are slippery and there
is a great deal of seaweed (not that dogs care about a little
seaweed). Be careful when disembarking and subsequently

reloading your pets, as Montsweag Road is fairly well traveled and there is no designated parking area. Do not park on private property. Check for ticks in the spring and summer after visiting this preserve.

Directions: Take U.S. Route 1 North through Bath and across the bridge (Kennebec River) to Woolwich. Stay on U.S. Route 1 North for 4.8 miles. Montsweag Road comes abruptly in from the right; take this sharp hairpin right-hander. Stay on Montsweag Road exactly 1.2 miles. The preserve is on your left. On the right is a large white house. Look for a small yellow sign on the telephone pole marked #57. The trailhead is very hard to spot. I recommend turning around in a driveway along Montsweag Road and then parking off the pavement (as best you can) near the aforementioned telephone pole (with the yellow Nature Conservancy sign). Look into the dense woods for the royal blue trail marker. As you enter the woods, you will see a wooden sign indicating this as Montsweag Preserve; it has a "loosely drawn" schematic of the trail. It might be good to bring a compass or GPS unit, but it is not entirely necessary.

Mount Ararat School (Topsham)

Overall Score	🐾🐾	Difficulty	🔥 🔥
Average Time	30 mins.–1+ hr	Parking	🦴🦴🦴
Average Distance	1–4 miles	Trail Markings	★

This area offers a conglomeration of narrow paved roadway, sandy all-terrain vehicle (ATV) single-tracks, rough and rocky trails, and packed dirt. These woods are utilized by cross-country runners from the school, locals with or without pets, and ATV or snowmobile riders (in the winter). On any given day you will run into deer, wild turkey, and other humans. The majority of visitors do not bring pets, but pets are allowed everywhere except on the athletic fields.

There are several parking areas to choose from, all paved and near one of many trailheads. You would be wise to bring a GPS unit or compass here, because not all the trails are marked and the frequency with which they crisscross and intersect can be confusing, and it is easy to get disoriented. In the late summer there are lovely blueberries and blackberries to snack on. Please clean up after your pets by bringing your own poop bags. It might not be a bad idea to bring a leash to utilize to and from the parking area (which requires crossing the main road into and out of the school area) or when you meet runners. Most of the free/open-areas are behind the school or on the northeast side of the athletic fields. Please respect the school's posted signs.

Directions: Take the Topsham exit off U.S. Route 1 or Exit 31 off Interstate 295. You want to go to the intersection of Route 196 (east/west) and Route 201 (north/south). From Bath you can take the first exit for Topsham and travel up Route 196 N to this intersection. From Brunswick take Maine Street to the end and go over the bridge past the Sea Dog Brewery; this is now Route 201 N. From the intersection of routes 196 and 201 take Route 201 N, and you will immediately encounter the sign (on the right side of the road) for Mount Ararat School. Enter here and follow the road to the athletic fields or to the back of the school buildings to get to a trailhead.

Noble Hill Preserve (Phippsburg)

Overall Score	🐾	Difficulty	🔥
Average Time	30 mins.	Parking	None
Average Distance	0.8 miles	Trail Markings	None

A small, short out-and-back trail but still a neat area to walk your dogs. If your pets are prone to chasing anything, especially horses, this is not the place for you. This property runs alongside a large horse farm, and the only thing separating the horses from parts of the trail is a three-rail white fence. This preserve also has deer, so be prepared to have to chase down your dogs if they tend to pursue wildlife. The path starts out as a wide dirt packed walkway until you reach the white fence of the Noble Hill Horse Farm; there the trail narrows. There are no tree markers or maps, but the trail direction is self-explanatory. You can walk down to the water, and by keeping the horse fence on your

right you will end up at a public boat launch into the Kennebec River. This is a privately donated piece of property, and it does run between homes and privately owned properties, so please obey all signs, bring your own cleanup bags, and keep your dogs under control at all times.

Directions:

Take U.S. Route 1 to Bath. Coming from the south on U.S. Route 1, get off at the second exit in Bath, High Street/ Phippsburg, and go right at the top of the ramp. This is High Street, a.k.a. Route 209 South. Stay on Route 209 S for 3.9 miles. If you are coming into Bath from the north, exit U.S. Route 1 in Bath and follow the road under the overpass; you will see signs for Route 209 South. Make a left under the overpass, in front of the Bath post office. This left is onto Washington Street, travel 2 miles to the intersection of Washington Street and Route 209 S. Go left and stay on Route 209 S for 2.1 miles. Go left on Fiddlers Reach Road. The pavement ends after

1.3 miles, and the preserve is almost immediately on your right (after the road turns to dirt). Park off the main road as best you can without blocking the gate to the preserve. There is no official parking area.

Mud Pond Nature Preserve (North Windham)

Honorable Mention

This is a small preserve that gives you an out-and-back stroll down to Mud Pond. It has a well-kept trail, and the views of the pond and the surrounding woods are lovely. The mosquitoes and flies are quite dense in the summer months, so bring bug spray for yourself and your pets. There are no maps or informational kiosk, and surrounding properties are privately owned, so stay on the trail. People sometimes use this walk as a nice lunch-break stroll. The parking area is small, but it is off the roadway. Please bring your own poop bags and clean up after your pets.

Directions: You have to get to Route 302 West out of Portland. There are several ways to do this; the easiest may be via Exit 48 off I-95 (traveling from the north or south). Follow the signs for Route 302—you will be on Riverside Street (north) for about 1 mile after you come off I-95. Once you are on Route 302 West, you will travel a total of 11.6 (a little more) miles. Mile markers are as follows: At 5.9 miles you'll pass Albion Road; at 7.4 miles you will come to a large roundabout representing the intersection of Routes 302/202/4; at 10 miles you will come to the intersection of Routes 35 and 115. Keep going and take a right on Anglers Road (a dirt road). This road is marked as private, but you can drive on it to get to the preserve. Watch the speed limit and go slowly between the homes and camps. Go 0.4 mile and then veer right onto Woodland Road; you are following the signs for the public boat launch. After 0.6 mile Woodland Road becomes Mt. Hunger Shores Road; after another 0.7+ mile you will see the preserve parking area and sign on the right.

Ovens Mouth Preserve (Boothbay/Dover)

Overall Score	🐾🐾🐾	Difficulty	🔥
Average Time	1–2.5 hrs.	Parking	🦴🦴🦴
Average Distance	1–4.5 miles	Trail Markings	★★★

A lovely collection of trails near the popular Boothbay Harbor region. This land trust is owned and maintained by the Boothbay Region Land Trust (BRLT). It encompasses 146 acres, and dogs are permitted off-leash as long as they are kept under control. There are two loops separated by a salt marsh. You can park by the western trail system (off Dover Cross Road) and enjoy three different trails

totaling 3 miles. The eastern trail system is off the Dover Road Extension and has about 1.6 miles to explore. The trails are hard-packed dirt, and since most run alongside water, there are some terrific views of either Back River or Ovens Mouth River. The terrain is varied; all in all these trails are flat and easy to navigate. The trails are well marked with different-colored tree blazes. There are informational kiosks at both parking areas, and free maps are available. In my opinion, the maps are descriptive and accurate but not to scale. This preserve is open all year, with the summer months being the busiest, since there are so many visitors to the Boothbay region. Please bring your own poop bags and clean up after your pets.

Directions: Take U.S. Route 1 North from Brunswick (off Exit 28 on Interstate 295 North or South), travel through Bath and over the bridge across the Kennebec River (past Bath Iron Works) into Woolwich. Reset the mile counter on your car as you come across the bridge and travel on U.S. Route 1 for a total of 10.5 miles. Following signs toward Boothbay, go right on Route 27 South (a.k.a. Wiscasset Road). After 7 miles on Route 27 S, there is a small sign for Ovens Mouth Preserve pointing to the right. Go right on Dover Road. Continue 2.4 miles, and you will be on Dover Road Extension, which will dead end. Parking is right here on the left; the trailhead is to the right. To get to the west preserve, after 1.9 miles on Dover Road (after the right-hand turn off Route 27), go left on Dover Cross Road. After 0.2 mile you will see the small parking area and informational kiosk on the right side of the road. The trailhead is dead ahead.

Peacock Beach State Park (Gardiner)

Honorable Mention

This park is only open between Memorial Day and Labor Day, but you can park at the gate and walk down to the picnic area and Pleasant Pond. If you have snowshoes and dogs that love basking in the white stuff, mid-winter is an excellent time to come. In the summer this place charges admission and there are lots of humans. Dogs have to be on a leash in the summer. If you wanted to take the family on an outing, launch a boat, have a cookout, or enjoy a freshwater pond, come on down with the pooches and the family when the park is open. There is a nice little beach, toilet facilities, and a large parking area. A lifeguard is on duty in the summer months. You must clean up after your pets, so bring poop bags (and leashes if it's not off-season).

Directions: Peacock Beach State Park is located off Route 201 South on Pleasant Pond in Richmond, about 12 miles from Augusta. Take Interstate 295 North to

the last exit before the merge of I-295 and I-95 (Gardiner). Or take I-95 South past Augusta to the intersection of I-295 and I-95, then continue on I-295 to the first exit, Route 201/Gardiner. Follow signs for Route 201 South. Staying on Route 201 South about 1.9 miles, Peacock Beach State Park is on the right side of the road as you head towards Richmond Corner. The park itself spans both sides of Route 201.

Pedestrian Bridge (Brunswick/Topsham)

Honorable Mention

A very short little jaunt along the Androscoggin River. This is a good place for dogs to take a dip on a warm day. The river runs quite rapidly, so keep an eye on your charges. Overall this area will not give you more than 0.5 mile of walking, but it's easy to find and accessible from the Topsham or Brunswick side of the Androscoggin River. If you come over the pedestrian bridge from Brunswick, keep your dogs on leashes until you get to the trailhead. The trail is hard-packed dirt, and down by the river it's sandy. Bring your own poop bags and clean up your pet's waste. The areas around the parking lots (on both sides) are paved, as are small walking paths leading away from the bridge. The parking areas are nice, but be aware that you are near very busy roads, so do not let your pets off-leash until you get onto the dirt path on the Topsham side.

Directions: Follow U.S. Route 1 South into Brunswick. The pedestrian bridge is directly off U.S. Route 1 on the right side of the road. There is a small parking area, and you will see the reddish bridge spanning the river. Park here and walk with your pets across the river, then veer to the right on the other side. The trailhead is on the right-end of the parking area on the Topsham side of the river. If you are coming from the south, take Exit 28 off Interstate 295 and follow signs for U.S. Route 1 North. Take the first exit off U.S Route 1, Topsham/Route 201/Route 24. Take Maine

Street across the bridge, passing the Seadog Brewing Company. Immediately go left on Summer Street. Travel 0.4 mile on Summer Street, then go left on Bridge Street;. 0.2 mile down Bridge Street on the left is the parking area for this pedestrian bridge. The trail leads into the woods and along the river to the left side of the parking area. Do not cross the bridge if you are already on the Topsham side— unless you want to, of course.

Philip Mailly Park (Bowdoinham)

Honorable Mention

Easy to access! A place to take your pooch for a quick dip or a rest from being in the car. Please bring your own poop bags and clean up after your pets. There are picnic tables, access to the Cathance River, a boat launch, and a pretty railroad bridge. The parking area is large, and there is a small coffee shop and store nearby. Please respect other patrons who may be using the park.

Directions: This park is at the intersection of Route 24 North and Route 138/125 East/West in downtown Bowdoinham. Coming north on Route 24 from Topsham, you will pass the park on your right. Coming east on Route 138/125 (they are the same road for a bit), you will hit Route 24 in front of the Bowdoinham market; go either straight or right onto Route 24, and the park is immediately on your left.

Pineland (East Gray/West Pownal)

Overall Score	🐾🐾🐾	Difficulty	🔥🔥🔥
Average Time	1–2 hrs.	Parking	🦴🦴
Average Distance	1.7–3.5 miles	Trail Markings	★★

A magnificent find not far from the acclaimed Pineland Estate (which no longer allows dogs). Two different trails add up to over 3.5 miles of exploring. Areas that are wet have been equipped with man-made bridges or large logs to walk on. This is designated State of Maine Public Reserve

Land, near the Royal River. In places tree roots make the walking a bit of a challenge, so wear good shoes. It is quiet, and there is a lot to see and explore. At one point you come down to the bank of the Royal River (if you are on the northern loop) near a railroad bridge. The trail is marked, but at times the marks are very spaced out or hard to see; however, because this trail varies from wide to very wide, it is easy to follow. People with dogs come here a great deal, since Pineland Estate no longer allows dogs on the property. The patrons I have met have had their pets leashed, but I think this was personal preference. There is an informational kiosk, but no free maps. The northern loop starts right from the parking area and the southern loop starts in the woods along the northern loop trail. Bring your own poop bags for excrement cleanup.

Directions: Finding this preserve can be difficult. The easiest is to come from Gray. Out of Gray take Yarmouth Road/ Route 115 East for a little over 1 mile. Go left on Depot Road (in East Gray). Stay on Depot Road for a little over 2 miles, and the preserve parking area is on your left. You will see the sign hanging out toward the street right before you see the parking lot and the informational kiosk. (Not that much information is posted on this kiosk, and there is no map.)

From Yarmouth, at exit 17 off Interstate 295, for example, you will go south on U.S. Route 1 until it intersects with Route 115 W. Take Route 115 W through North Yarmouth, and then (veering slightly to the right) take Route 231

North/West out of North Yarmouth toward New Glouces-
ter. In Pineland go left on Depot Road (it is called Allen
Road if you go right on it), and the preserve is 0.5 mile up
and on your right.

From Portland or points south take Interstate 95 north to
Gray and Exit 63. Then go east on Route 115 and follow
the directions above from Gray.

From Freeport, follow signs and drive as though going to
Bradbury Mountain State Park, but in Pownal Center, at
the intersection of Elmwood Road and Route 9, go straight
(not right on Route 9 to Bradbury) and continue west on
Elmwood Road. Elmwood Road Ts with Allen Road; go left
here. Allen Road intersects with Route 231, Morse Road,
and Depot Road at the same time. Veer slightly left onto
Depot Road, crossing Route 231. The preserve is ahead
about 0.5 mile on your right off Depot Road.

Pratt's Brook Park (Yarmouth)

Overall Score	🐾🐾🐾	Difficulty	🔥🔥
Average Time	1–2 hrs.	Parking	🦴🦴🦴
Average Distance	1–3.8 miles	Trail Markings	★★

A delightful place that offers a slew of trails that inter-
mingle and crisscross and have the potential to entertain
for a couple of hours. This is a cross-country ski area in the

winter, but during
the summer it is
a lovely place to
walk dogs off-leash.
There are 10 differ-
ent trails to choose
from. All trails start
out in a big field;
some are mown
portions through
the tall grass, which
then go into the

woods. The trails all have animal names: Bear Briar is 1.4 miles long and takes about 35 minutes to complete; Moose Meander is 1.4 miles long and takes 40 minutes; Otter Overlook takes you down to a stream where dogs can get wet; Coyote Crossing comes off Moose Meander; and it is 0.7 mile long and takes about 13 minutes. Rabbit Run, Chipmunk Cache, Raccoon Ramble, Deer Divide, Fox Folly, and Skunk Stroll are the remaining trails, which intersect with one or more of the others; these trails are all less than 0.5 mile long and take around 5 to 15 minutes to traverse. The trail markers are up very high on the trees, probably to compensate for large amounts of snowfall. Not all trails are marked equally well, but most are very hard-packed dirt and over 3 feet wide, thus easy to follow. Clean up after your pets, bring your own poop bags, and be aware of mountain bikers. Please respect other patrons you may meet.

Directions: Take Interstate 295 either north or south to Exit 17 (just south of Freeport); this is the Yarmouth/Freeport exit. Take U.S. Route 1 South for 0.3 mile to East Main Street. Go right on East Main Street and then go immediately left on North Street. Stay on North  Street for 1.1 miles. Pratt's Brook Park is on the right side of the road. A small sign is posted directly in front of the turn into the parking area. The parking area is gravel, large in size, and located away from the traffic on North Street. Go to the informational sign to get an idea about the trails. Maps are not always available, so you may have to memorize the trail layout. In certain areas there are maps posted out on the trail.

Quarry Run Dog Park (Portland)

Overall Score	🐾🐾	Difficulty	🔥
Average Time	>15 mins.	Parking	🦴
Average Distance	0.4 miles	Trail Markings	None

A medium-sized off-leash dog park in Portland. Dogs and humans frequent this place at all hours of the day and in all kinds of weather. There is plenty of space here, and included are some walking trails. The entire property is fenced in. There is no map. The trails simply goes around the perimeter of the fenced-in area. This park was built on an old trash-dump site, so it was recommended to me that my dogs *not* drink the water that runs to the left of the entrance. If you walk straight to the back and top of the property there is a large, flat area where the dogs can romp and play. There is also a covered picnic-bench area. Remember, you are responsible for your own and others' safety, as well as the safety of all pets present. Usually there are bags provided for pet excrement cleanup, but it is always wise to bring your own as well.

Directions: Take the Washington Avenue exit in Portland off Interstate 295 (going north or south), and head west on Washington Ave until you reach Ocean Avenue. Go right on Ocean Avenue. Travel a little more than 1 mile, and the park is on your left. You will make a left and drive up an incline to the parking area. There is only a tiny sign

hanging on a chain link fence to indicate the park entrance. Once you crest the small incline, park on the left side nose in. Some people leash their dogs between their cars and the park's entry gate.

Reid State Park – *seasonal* (Georgetown)

Overall Score	🐾🐾🐾	Difficulty	🔥
Average Time	1–4 hrs.	Parking	🦴🦴🦴
Average Distance	>1.6 miles	Trail Markings	★

Many Maine State Parks do not allow dogs between April 1 and Sept. 30, and this is one of them. But if you can get here in the off-season, it is worth it. It is a large park with many trails; some are marked and some are not. Signs all over the park indicate that pets must be on a leash; however, in the off-season you hardly meet or see anyone else, so use your discretion. Poop bags are provided at some trailheads (not all). The trail that goes along the beach and around the outermost point has no trail markers and can be confusing to follow—it suddenly dead-ends at a picnic area or disappears into undergrowth. The beach is very

pretty. Please observe the signs posted regarding preservation of the beach dunes and staying on the posted walkways. Don't let your dogs drink too much salt water, as it can make them sick. If your dogs normally drink a lot of water on your regular walks, plan ahead and bring a portable bowl and some fresh water.

Directions: This is a large park, and there are many sources for directions in guide books, on maps, and on signs off U.S. Route 1. First take U.S. Route 1 to Bath and then continue north over the bridge across the Kennebec River. Veer to the right on the other side of the bridge and follow the signs to Route 127 South. If you are coming south on U.S. Route 1 from Wiscasset, follow the signs for Route 127 S (on the right side of the road immediately before the bridge across the Kennebec River toward Bath). Stay on Route 127 S through Georgetown; the road name will change to Five Islands Road. You stay on this road for a total of 10.6 miles from where you originally entered Route 127 S. There is a large sign indicating that you need to take a right onto Seguin Island Road in order to get to Reid State Park. After 1.3 miles you are on park property. Keep going until you reach the entrance. Slow down and please pay the fee even if there is no attendant.

Ridgewell Preserve (Phippsburg)

Overall Score	🐾🐾🐾	Difficulty	🔥 🔥
Average Time	1–3.5 hrs.	Parking	🦴
Average Distance	1–6 miles	Trail Markings	★★

Easy to find with a good trail map, varied terrain, and a good 3.5 hours worth of hiking if you take all the various loops that are available. This preserve encompasses 200 acres and four different colored trails (orange, white, red, and blue). A plastic-

covered map is stapled to a tree with an indicator of where you are located at every trail intersection (very convenient). The trails include the "dinosaur rocks," a Sequin Island overlook, a stone wall, swamps, creeks, and two ponds. The map that is available at the trailhead is fantastically accurate and descriptive. If you lose track of the trail markers, turn around and spot the tree blaze that is going in the opposite direction from where you are traveling. The mounting angle and location of the opposite direction blazes will guide you to where your next trail marker should be. Please bring your own poop bags and pick up after your dogs. Most of these trails are remote from roads or houses, so if you are worried about losing your way, take along a compass or GPS unit. Some trails traverse slippery rock faces or rutted woodland terrain, so wear appropriately rugged shoes.

Directions: Take U.S. Route 1 to Bath. Coming from the south on U.S. Route 1, get off at the second exit in Bath, High Street/Phippsburg, and go right at the top of the ramp. This is Route 209 S. Stay on Route 209 S for 10.1 (nearly 10.2) miles. If you are coming into Bath from the north, exit U.S. Route 1 in Bath and follow the road under the overpass; you will see signs for Route 209 S. Go left on Washington Street (underneath the overpass), which intersects with Route 209 S after 2 miles. Go left onto Route 209 S and travel for 8.3 (nearly 8.4) miles. Pride Rock Way is a small street (gravel) that comes in from your left. Take this left and park off the street as best you can. There is no designated parking area; it is actually an intersection of three dirt roads, so try not to block any of the roads. You might have to be creative with your parking. Just past the Ridgewell Preserve sign you will see the green box that contains the trail maps and a sign-in book.

Rines Forest (Cumberland/Northeast Falmouth)

Honorable Mention

The Rines Forest is a land trust (easement) of more than 216-acres in Cumberland near the Falmouth town line. It offers a variety of trails that include several waterfalls, a large wetland area on the eastern side of the property, stone walls, and dense woods everywhere. In the summer months bugs, mosquitoes, and no-see-ums are horrid, so bring repellent. On all sides this property abuts private residences, so please respect any and all "private property" signs. There is a map available for the public at the informational kiosk near Range Road. There is no formal parking area, so you have to park off the pavement as best you can. Because of the lack of parking and because this trailhead is so close to traffic, please be very careful when loading and unloading your pets. Please clean up after your pets; be responsible and bring your own poop bags to this walk.

Directions: Range Road runs between Route 100/26 (Portland Road) North/South and Route 9 (Longwoods Road) near Cumberland Center. If you are on Interstate 295, take Exit 10 and go briefly south on U.S. Route 1 (right off the exit). Go right (twice), ending up on Route 9 N. Stay on Route 9 N for about 3 miles, then go left on Range Road. A little over 1 mile on Range Road the preserve will appear on the right side of the roadway.

Coming south from Gray, take Route 100/26 South through West Cumberland and look for Range Road on the left. After turning left onto Range Road, travel approximately 1.5 miles, and the preserve is on the left side of the road.

Traveling north from Portland, take Exit 53 off Interstate 95 and continue north on Route 100/26. Range Road comes in from the right after about 4.5 miles. Go right on Range Road, and the preserve will be on the left about 1.5 miles down. Range Road intersects Winn Road, which also connects Route 100/26 and Route 9 (Falmouth to Cumberland). You can take Winn Road to Range Road; go left on Range Road and the preserve is 1 mile up on your right side.

"Road" under Power Lines (Wiscasset)

Honorable Mention

This is a wide, mown, grassy "road" that runs parallel to power lines near an old railroad track (which I believe is no longer in use, based on the amount of weeds growing up between the tracks). As a rule, State of Maine land that runs under power lines is an easement, which can be utilized for recreational purposes. This is a nice open space to take your dogs off-leash. As you walk up the hill away from your car on the 10-foot-wide mown road, keep the powerlines on your right. After cresting the hill the road goes into the woods and winds through the forest. Eventually you will come to a paved road. Go left at this paved road and walk down the hill to the end; here there is a boat ramp going into the Back River (part of the Sheepscot River). If so inclined your pooches can take a dip in the salty-brackish water. Go back the same way you came. This walk takes about 1 hour. Be aware that some dogs react to power lines and electrically charged air. So watch your pets for signs, such as tucking their tails, shivering or shaking, or

simply stopping and not wanting to go further. If any of your pets exhibit this sort of behavior, do not continue on this walk. You will be parking rather close to Route 144, so be careful when unloading and loading your off-leash pets from your vehicle, so they do not run into the street.

Directions: You have to get to Brunswick, so take Interstate 295 North out of Portland or South from Augusta, and take Exit 28. Continuing north on U.S. Route 1 from Brunswick through Bath, go over the bridge across the Kennebec River (past Bath Iron Works) and into Woolwich. Reset the mile counter on your car as you come across the bridge; you will be traveling on U.S. Route 1 North for a total of 5.8 (nearly 5.9) miles. Go right on Route 144, and travel a total of 1.5 miles. After 0.8 (nearly 0.9) mile, Route 144 makes a 90-degree turn to the left, take this left and keep going a total of 1.5 miles on Route 144. You will see the power lines overhead and the dirt/grass road on your right off the pavement. There is a gate across the road; park off to the side as best you can so you do not block the gate, and walk from here.

Robert Tristram Coffin Flower Fields (Woolwich)

Overall Score	🐾🐾	Difficulty	🔥
Average Time	30 mins.	Parking	🦴
Average Distance	0.5 miles	Trail Markings	★★

Who can resist flowers, views of Merrymeeting Bay and a quiet walk in the woods? The New England Wildflower

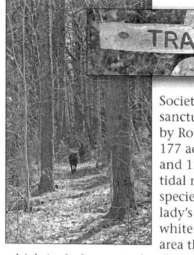

Society owns this wildflower sanctuary. This sanctuary is split by Route 128, but it encompasses 177 acres of hilly woods, a brook, and 1256 feet of sandy shore and tidal marsh. Over 100 wildflower species exist here, including pink lady's slipper, yellow violet, and white baneberry. By the parking area there is a little map box, which includes a guestbook and maps of the areas that are owned by the Wildflower Society. There is also an extremely rudimentary map of the short 0.5-mile walking trail that parallels Merrymeeting Bay. The trail is marked with paint on the trees in addition to round, metal, green and white markers that identify this as a New England Wildflower Society property. It is an easy-to-follow trail. Please clean up after your pets by bringing your own poop bags.

Note: It is not entirely clear whether you can or cannot bring dogs to this location. It is a short trail that makes a nice loop, so go early to stay away from the bugs in the summertime. Just be aware of flower lovers who may not be too keen on your dogs!

Directions: Take U.S. Route 1 North to Woolwich (coming over the bridge from Bath). Go left on Route 127 North. Go about 1.8 miles and take another left on Route 128 North. Stay on Route 128 North for 4.7 miles. Chopps Point Road comes in from the left, but this sanctuary is actually straight ahead, as Route 128 veers right. There is a small parking area on your left immediately north of a blue sign for "Chops Crossing" with a path leading to the right just behind the entrance. The entrance sign is white and identifies this as the Robert Tristam Coffin Flower Fields.

Rocky Hill (Bath)

Overall Score	🐾🐾🐾	Difficulty	🔥🔥
Average Time	50 mins.–1 hr.	Parking	Off-street
Average Distance	1.7 miles	Trail Markings	None

This little gem is located near the Career Center in Bath. You will be walking on a road that was created by big-rig trucks while they were tearing down an old water tower that was located at the top of Rocky Hill. The road that you walk on away from your car, through a field and eventually up Rocky Hill, will fork a few times and you will have some choices to make. If at the first intersection you choose to go right, you can walk on the trails that progress under the power lines. However, if at the crest of the hill you continue straight, you will be in the woods for a while until the trail starts curving sharply to the left and goes down a steep and rocky descent. This is the indicator that you should turn around and go back the same way you came. When you get back to the aforementioned intersection, go north (left); the road will take you to the area where the Rocky Hill water tank used to be. It is now a big, flat concrete slab. Here, you will have to turn around and head back down. Doing all these short out-and-back excursions should keep you and your pets busy for a solid hour. It may be a good idea to bring a compass or GPS unit.

Directions: Take the Congress Avenue exit off U.S. Route 1 in Bath. Go right twice off the exit ramp if you are coming from the south; go right only once if you are exiting from the north. You are now on Congress Avenue. Continue on Congress Avenue for approximately 0.4 mile. You will come to the intersection of Centre Street and Congress Avenue—there is a single traffic light here that only turns on if someone wishes to cross the street. Go left onto Centre Street (following the signs for the Career Center). Travel a mere 0.1 mile, and you will see a road (dirt and gravel) going off into a large field on the left side of the road. Turn around and park off the pavement here. Be careful when loading and unloading your dogs, because this can be a busy street. Walk on the rudimentary road away from your vehicle and up Rocky Hill.

Rogers Neck Hill (Phippsburg)

Overall Score	🐾 🐾	Difficulty	🔥
Average Time	50 mins.–1 hr.	Parking	🦴
Average Distance	1.3 miles	Trail Markings	None

As with some of the other properties in this book, these are not trails per se; they are rather ATV or snowmobile trails or old logging roads. They are wide and easy to follow, but not marked. In order to explore the area, I recommend bringing a compass or GPS unit, so you can safely find your way back to your vehicle. Trails like these do abut

private properties and sometimes homes, so if you really did feel lost you could likely find someone to ask for directions. But it is better to have your own directional aids. There are some inclines here, but nothing too strenuous. Rogers Neck Hill is located to your right as you walk southward and slightly east of where you parked. Eventually you will have walked all the way down to Rogers Neck Road. There is a pond on this peninsula, Rogers Neck Pond, but it does not have easy access—it is very overgrown. There is a wetland and swamp area on the southern point of your walk, so stay on the roads/trails. The mosquitoes are very plentiful in the summer months. When in doubt, simply go back the same way you came.

Directions: Take U.S. Route 1 to Bath. Coming from the south, get off at the second exit in Bath, High Street/ Phippsburg, and go right at the top of the ramp. This is High Street, a.k.a. Route 209 South. Stay on Route 209 S for 4.1 miles. If you are coming into Bath from the north, exit U.S. Route 1 in Bath as you come over the Kennebec River bridge; follow the road under the overpass, where you will see signs for Route 209 S. Make a left under the overpass. This left is onto Washington Street, which intersects with Route 209 South after 2 miles. Go left onto Route 209 S, and travel 2.3 miles. Go left on Fiddlers Reach Road. Take the very next right onto Old Ferry Road; this is a dirt road. Stay on Old Ferry Road for 0.4 mile. Go right onto Cold Spring Farm Road, then travel a mere 0.2 or 0.3 mile and you will see outcroppings off the roadway where you can park (on the right side). If you park 0.2 or 0.3 mile down Cold Spring Farm Road, either trail will take you up toward Rogers Neck Hill.

Royal River Park—Picnic Point— Dog Off-Leash Area (Yarmouth)

Overall Score	🐾 🐾 🐾	Difficulty	N/A
Average Time	>30 mins.	Parking	🦴
Average Distance	park & river	Trail Markings	None

A very well kept, nicely situated official off-leash park. Poop bags are provided, as are several trash barrels for disposal purposes. There is a paved path that leads down to the river. Dogs can swim, romp on the grass, or just sniff around. In other sections of the park (south of the dog area) there are restricted times when dogs can be present, but at this off-leash area dogs can come during all daylight hours. Town ordinance requires that feces must be removed immediately and that dogs be kept under control. The parking area is small and very close to the road, so be careful when unloading and loading your pets. The park is not fenced in, but the river provides a nice barrier on two sides. The entire park is only about 4 to 5 acres.

Directions: Take Interstate 295 North from Portland or South from Freeport to Exit 17. Interstate 295 intersects with U.S. Route 1 here; go south on U.S. Route 1, 0.9 (nearly 1.0) mile into Yarmouth town center. Go right (north) on Main Street (a.k.a. Route 115 N) for 0.3 mile. After 0.3 mile Main Street intersects with East and West Elm Street; go right onto East Elm Street. After 0.2 mile you will cross railroad tracks. Immediately after crossing the railroad tracks the parking area is on your right. If you cross

over the river (on a small bridge) you have gone too far. The parking area is only a sliver of gravel/dirt on the south side of East Elm Street.

Sam Moore Road Power Lines (North Woolwich/South Dresden)

Honorable Mention

Off busy Route 127 but still worth a stop if you and your pooches need a place to wander around off-leash near Woolwich. This is a rocky but lovely ATV track that runs under the power lines between Routes 127 and 128. It goes out and back for a round trip of about 4 miles. There are no trail markers or maps, but the track is well utilized (packed dirt or rocky) and easy to follow (other than navigating all the loose rocks). There is a small parking area off the road, which allows you to unload and load your pets fairly safely. Bring a compass or GPS unit in case you wander off too far, so you can get back to your vehicle. If your dogs have any physical limitations, this is probably not the best trail for you. Wear good shoes so you don't run the risk of spraining your ankle.

Directions: Only a few miles from the intersection of U.S. Route 1 and Route 127 North out of Woolwich. Take U.S. Route 1 North past Bath over the bridge across the Kennebec River and into Woolwich. Go 0.3 mile past the bridge and then left onto Route 127 N. Go approximately 3.8 miles, and Sam Moore Road is on your left as you approach the giant power-line overpass across Route 127. Turn left onto Sam Moore Road and then park off the road on the left; walk east under the power lines.

Sayles Field (Freeport)

Overall Score	🐾🐾🐾	Difficulty	🔥
Average Time	1–2.5 hrs.	Parking	Off-street
Average Distance	1–5 miles	Trail Markings	★★★

Here there are some large areas with mown paths that create a perimeter around and through enjoyable fields. As you traverse the fields, you will enter the woods; the trails are well marked and well maintained. This is varied terrain with packed dirt trails. The white trail is the longest and seemingly most utilized. A blue trail traverses the white trail and allows you to make a loop if you wish. There are several wet spots, some brook crossings, and some wetlands or swampy areas. Mosquitoes are very dense, as are horseflies, in the summer months. You can walk from Sayles Field to the Bliss Woods Preserve (off S. Freeport Road) and back. This property is owned and maintained by the Freeport Conservation Trust and encompasses 72 acres. The preserve borders Pine Street and Church Road. Lots of people bring their dogs here, and the majority are off-leash. There is a large trash can and clean poop bags for the taking to make it easier for visitors to pick up after their pets. Be alert and a responsible pet owner when you meet others on this trail.

Directions: Travel on Interstate 295 to Freeport and take Exit 20, Desert Road/Freeport. Go toward Freeport as you come off the ramp. At the first light, go right (which is south) onto U.S. Route 1. Then immediately take the next left, Pine Street. Stay on Pine Street for 1.4 miles. Church Road is the last right-hand turn off Pine Street before it intersects with S. Freeport Road (which is a four-way stop). Church Road is a narrow dirt road, which has houses on both sides. The preserve is squeezed between two homes, so you have to park on the side of the road without blocking any driveways or intruding on any lawns. Walk into the bushes to the right of the informational sign, and the fields open up in front of you. Go straight ahead through these fields to get to the trail system hidden in the woods. No trail map exists, so bringing a compass or GPS unit isn't a bad idea. As of the Fall 2008 it was suggested that dog owners keep their pets on a leash from the parking area until you enter the second large field.

Sewall Pond Conservation Area (Arrowsic/Georgetown)

Overall Score	🐾🐾	Difficulty	🔥
Average Time	20 mins.–1 hr.	Parking	🦴
Average Distance	0.6 + miles	Trail Markings	None

A great place for canine romping in or out of the freshwater pond. The main trail is wide and spacious for your dogs to run around off-leash. It is about 0.3 mile from where you park to the water's edge (Sewall Pond). There are no maps and no trail markings, so keep your bearings so you can get back to your car. There are short trails that veer off to the left and right from the main trail; these are out-and-back jaunts. The water is clean and clear and invites water-loving dogs with its gentle lapping on the rocks. In the winter this lake is frozen solid. It does not take long to explore this small preserve, but if you sit down on the rocks and let the dogs run around and play, plenty of time will go by. Please bring your own poop bags and clean up after yourself and your pets. It is not permitted to build fires in this area. Leave only footprints behind.

Directions: Take U.S. Route 1 from Brunswick north through Bath and continue over the bridge to Woolwich. In Woolwich bear right, going south on Route 127 (toward Georgetown). If you are coming from the north, head south on U.S. Route 1; take the right-hand exit before the bridge to Bath (across the Kennebec River) and catch Route 127 South (watch for signs for Reid State Park). On Route 127 S drive 1.7 miles, and you will see a white building on the left side of the road; this is the Arrowsic Town Hall. Go left immediately before the town-hall building onto Old Stage Road. Go 2.3 miles on Old Stage Road. This is a windy road with a 30-mph speed limit. Passing the Arrowsic Island Pottery (on your left) after 1.7 miles; continue on Old Stage Road until you reach the conservation area, which will be on your right. Look for the large wooden sign with dark green writing or the small white signs nailed to the trees that identify the conservation area boundary. Parking is limited, and for the most part it is alongside the road (slightly off the pavement). There are some small gravel outcroppings along the right side of the street that you can use if they are not occupied. Do not park on the left side of the road as you approach the conservation area—there are a multitude of "private property—you will be towed" signs posted here!

Sewall Woods (Bath)

Overall Score	🐾 🐾	Difficulty	🔥 🔥
Average Time	45 mins.–1.5 hrs	Parking	🦴 🦴
Average Distance	0.7–2.1 miles	Trail Markings	★ ★

This is a little-used preserve where dogs are allowed. It is managed by the Lower Kennebec Regional Land Trust. There is one primary loop trail that is marked with light blue paint on the trees and small wooden signs. This trail is less than 1 mile long, but there are a wide variety of other trails you can utilize. If you continue straight where the blue trail starts looping back, you will end up on the back side of the Bath dump. From here you can walk down to the Kennebec River. Then you can follow the trail that runs north along the riverbank. It is 0.7 mile from the parking area to the water's edge. In total you can wander up the river and come back the same way, logging over 2 miles. It is possible to walk so far (skirting the river's edge) that you end up on trails at the Thorne Head Preserve, and then you have about 4 miles of walking to get back. Please bring your own poop bags and do not remove anything from the woods.

Note: This is an area where it is permitted to hunt, so in the fall it is a good idea that both you and your dogs wear blaze orange. Vests for your pooches can be purchased online or at L.L. Bean® in Freeport.

Directions: Take U.S. Route 1 north to Bath, exiting at High Street/Phippsburg; go left onto High Street (heading north). If you are coming from the north, exit U.S. Route 1 as you come off the bridge over the Kennebec River and go straight down the hill to the first light. Go right here; this is Washington Street. At the next light go left on Center Street and up the hill to High Street. At High Street go right—the Androscoggin County Court House and Sheriff's Office are on the left corner at this intersection. Stay on High Street going north for 1.6 miles. Go left onto Whiskeag Road. The entrance to Sewall Woods is on your right less than 0.2 mile from the intersection. Pull up the gravel incline through the stone pillars to the small parking area near the Sewall Woods informational kiosk. Follow the trailhead off into the woods here, or you can opt to walk up the dirt road that goes to a torn-down water-tower area and pick up trails from there. Trail maps are available, but they are very inaccurate. If you plan on going off the marked trail, bring a compass or GPS unit.

Skolfield Shores Preserve (Harpswell)

Overall Score	🐾🐾🐾	Difficulty	🔥
Average Time	45 mins.–1 hr.	Parking	🦴🦴
Average Distance	1–1.8 miles	Trail Markings	★★★

This is not a very large preserve, but the trails are fun and there are 4400 feet of shorefront. The trail system (there are three separate trails that make interconnected loops) runs in between some houses, a large farm, and land near the farm. Please do not allow your dogs to run onto any of these private properties. This preserve encompasses 19 acres. The trails are well marked and easy to follow. There is a place where you can go down to the water and the dogs can go swimming. Be aware of the sharp shells and rocks that are present at this water entry. One of the trails' main attractions is the large man-made bridges. They provide unique opportunities for pictures that are framed naturally by the angular architecture. The bigger bridges are along the Hemlock Trail. Several places along the trails have benches for humans to rest and look at the view while the pups romp around. Please bring your own poop bags and clean up after your pets. There is a map at the parking area's information kiosk.

Directions: Take U.S. Route 1 from Bath or Brunswick to the Cooks Corner Exit. Upon exiting, get into the far right-hand lane and turn right at the first large intersection (following signs to Brunswick Naval Air Station); this is Bath Road. Stay on Bath Road for 2.2 miles. As you approach the intersection of Route 123 South

and Bath Road, stay in the left lane and go left onto Route 123 S. This is Sills Road; on some in-vehicle GPS systems it becomes Harpswell Road. Continue on Route 123 S for 4.3 miles. You will see a large white farmhouse on a hill on your right. Skolfield Place is a dirt road that comes in from your right and goes up toward the large farmhouse. Parking is on the right (off Route 123), directly after the intersection of Route 123 S and Skolfield Place in a gravel lot. The parking area is fairly large, but do be careful when letting your dogs out of the car, as you are close to the busy road.

Sligo Road Recreation Area (Yarmouth)

Honorable Mention

Not an "official" hiking area per se but still a good open-space recreation area that is enjoyable for off-leash exercise. There is a wood-chip trail that leads away from the parking area. It takes you into a wooded area and eventually down toward the Royal River. Directly across the Royal River from this Sligo Road Recreation Area is Barker Lot, which also belongs to the town of Yarmouth and is a public-use open-space. To get over to Barker Lot, however, you would have to cross the river. There is no loop or marked trail system here, so bringing a compass or a GPS unit would be a good idea. In the summer the grassy field where you park is a good spot to pick up ticks, so take a good look at your dogs when you return home. Bring your own poop bags and carry out what you take in with you.

Directions: Take I-295 North from Portland or I-295 South from Freeport to Exit 17. Interstate

295 intersects with U.S. Route 1, so after coming off Exit 17, go south on U.S. Route 1 into Yarmouth town center (nearly 1 mile). Route 115 North, also called Main Street, is a right-hand turn. Go right (north) on Main Street for 0.5 mile. West Main Street will veer left, and Sligo Road will come down from the right (almost straight ahead). Drive onto Sligo Road and continue for 0.3 (nearly 0.4) mile. Immediately after you cross a set of railroad tracks, the Sligo Road Recreation Area is on your right. The parking lot is gravel. There is no informational kiosk or other indicator that this is the correct place, but you will see the wood-chip trail leading into the woods to the north/northeast.

Sortwell Memorial Forest (Wiscasset)

Overall Score	🐾🐾🐾	Difficulty	🔥 🔥
Average Time	1–2 hrs.	Parking	🦴🦴🦴
Average Distance	1–4 miles	Trail Markings	★

A true find not far from downtown Wiscasset. This is a 90-acre property owned and maintained by the New England Forestry Foundation. The property is shaped liked a large rectangle, with one long side runs parallel to Willow Lane. The trails are part

New England Forestry Foundation
www.NewEnglandForestry.org
Sortwell Memorial Forest
Donated 1955

of the Wiscasset Combined Trail System, where walking trails and snowmobile trails overlap and intersect. There are several trails to choose from; they aren't marked on a continuous basis, but there are indicators when the trail changes direction or splits—laminated signs on some trees

will help guide you. This is a fabulous place to take off-leash dogs. Wild turkeys roost here, and deer live in the woods. There are several brook or river crossings, so after a rainfall it is quite wet. This is varied terrain, and most of the time you are in dense woods. In the summer months insects are quite extreme. Because of all the wildlife and the narrow trails, keep your pets fairly close; if they run off, recall them sooner rather than later. There are pink or white streamers on several of the trees, so it is easy to follow the trail.

Directions: Off Interstate 295 take U.S. Route 1 North through Brunswick and Bath, then over the bridge across the Kennebec River (past Bath Iron Works) and into Woolwich. Reset the mile counter on your car as you come across the bridge and travel on U.S. Route 1 for a total of 9 miles. Go left on Route 27 in Wiscasset. Travel 0.3 mile north on Route 27 and then go left on Hooper Street. Go immediately left again on Churchill Street, then quickly go right on Willow Lane. There are several places along Willow Lane to pick up these trails, but the official parking area (gravel) is 0.7 mile up on the right. You will see the sign for Sortwell Memorial Forest. Bring your own poop bags. There is no informational kiosk or map, so a compass or GPS unit is not a bad idea even though the trails are reasonably easy to follow.

Spar Cove Forest (Freeport)

Overall Score	🐾🐾	Difficulty	🔥
Average Time	25–35 mins.	Parking	Off-street
Average Distance	1 mile	Trail Markings	★★

A small little conglomeration of trails that allows for a quick walk in the woods near Freeport and Interstate 295. The trails are hard-packed dirt, and there are some fallen trees that you have to maneuver around. There is some up-and-down hiking, and in places the trail goes past private homes, so if your dogs tend to run into other people's yards looking for cats to chase, be aware of this. The trail winds its way down to Spar Cove, which is part of the Harraseeket River. You can make a small loop, but you will end up coming back on parts of the same trail that you took when leaving your car. Please bring your own poop bags and clean up after your pets. Part of the trail (if you make the aforementioned loop) goes close to Staples Point Road, but the foliage and trees are dense here, so hopefully your canines won't spot something and decide to run into the road; nonetheless, be alert. Bug spray is a must if you visit here in the summer months.

Directions: To get here from north of Freeport, take Exit 20 off Interstate 295 S. Off the ramp head toward downtown Freeport, but at the first light go right onto U.S. Route 1 South. Take the very next left, Pine Street. Travel on Pine

Street for 1.4 miles until it comes to a four-way stop; take a right here onto S. Freeport Road. Travel a little over a mile on S. Freeport Road, then go left on Staples Point Road. This park is 0.5 mile further up and on the left (on a corner). If you are coming from the south on Interstate 295, take Exit 17, go north on U.S. Route 1 about 1 mile, turn right on South Freeport Road, then take another right after 0.3 mile onto Staples Point Road. Up Staples Point Road on the left (0.5 mile) is the off-road parking space.

Spirit Pond Preserve (Phippsburg)

Overall Score	🐾🐾🐾	Difficulty	🔥
Average Time	1–2 hrs.	Parking	🦴
Average Distance	2+ miles	Trail Markings	★★★

A Phippsburg Land Trust property that is well marked and provides 2 miles of walking in the woods near water and on great trails. The trail hugs the margin of Morse River. This area is not hilly or strenuous, and you will enjoy nice water views and a long shoreline. The trailhead is off to the left from where the green and yellow preserve sign is located; you will see the green box with trail maps hanging on a tree. In my opinion the trail map is accurate but not to scale. If you are pressed for time, you can make a shorter loop and return to your car by going up the single-track ATV road (making a 1-mile loop instead of the full

2 miles). Many offshoot trails allow you to walk down to the water, and your dogs can go swimming. Please respect the areas that are marked "private" on the map. As always, clean up after yourself and your pets by bringing your own plastic bags!

Directions: You can get to this preserve two different ways, but both require you to take U.S. Route 1 to Bath and exit at Phippsburg/High Street, then turn right, traveling south on Route 209. If you are coming from Wiscasset, exit U.S. Route 1 in Bath and take Washington Street (following the signs for Route 209 South) until you intersect with High Street. Go left heading south on Route 209. Stay on Route 209 as if you were going to Popham Beach. The trailhead is actually 0.3 mile back in the direction you are traveling from the sharp right-hand turn that Route 209 S makes when it intersects with Parker Head Road. But how do you measure 0.3 mile in the "backward" direction? Truth be told, the trailhead is on the south side (right) of Route 209, directly past the large sign (on the left) for Popham Woods (a new-home building site). Slow down after this sign and look to the right, and you should see the yellow and green preserve sign If you get to the 90-degree right-hand turn, you have gone too far.

An easier route is to take Parker Head Road south off Route 209 (it's a left-hand turn at Bisson's Market). Drive the entire length of Parker Head Road until you insect with Route 209. At this intersection go straight (onto Route 209 North) for 0.3 mile, and the trailhead and parking will be on the left side of the pavement. Be careful when pulling off the blacktop into the very small parking area, since traffic goes quite fast here. Also, watch your pets when you are near your car so they don't run out into traffic.

Sprague Pond (Phippsburg)

Overall Score	🐾🐾🐾	Difficulty	🔥 🔥
Average Time	1–2 hrs.	Parking	🦴
Average Distance	1–5.3 miles	Trail Markings	★★

Tough entry and exit, because the parking area is so close to the road, but there is lots to explore once you get through "the gauntlet." The first section of this preserve runs straight between two houses and private property. Thus, not even 3 feet off the trail, there are "private" signs, and 20 feet away you can see someone's home. These homes have other pets and "birds" (turkeys and large pheasants), which are very fun to chase if you are an off-leash dog. Therefore, this is one preserve where it is worth-while taking your leashes (with your dogs attached) for the first few hundred yards (until you are past the "gauntlet," so to speak). The trail is marked, but many of the white marks on the trees are a bit obscured by natural growth, so keep your wits about you. Bringing a compass or GPS unit is not a bad idea. The woods are dense, but once you spot Sprague Pond, you will realize the hike was well worth it. This is a very pretty, cozy lake. The trail goes along the perimeter of the lake, and at one point you have to cross a small brook. This is a great freshwater pond for swimming for both dogs and humans. For the most part the trail is fairly wide. In some places trees have fallen down, so you'll have to crawl over the fallen trees or go around. This is an out-and-back walk, so you have to return through the "gauntlet," which may mean leashing your pets again as you return to your vehicle. As always, please respect the preserve by cleaning up your own and your dogs' waste.

Directions: Take U.S. Route 1 to Bath. Coming from the south on U.S. Route 1, get off at the second exit in Bath, High Street/Phippsburg, and go right at the top of the ramp. This is Route 209 S. Stay on Route 209 South for 9.5 (nearly 9.6) miles. If you are coming into Bath from the north, exit U.S. Route 1 in Bath and follow the road under the overpass; you will see signs for Route 209 S. Go left on Washington Street (underneath the overpass), which intersects with Route 209 S after 2 miles. Go left onto Route 209 S and travel for 7.7 (nearly 7.8) miles. The rather small parking area for Sprague Pond is immediately off the pavement on your right. It is frightfully close to the very busy roadway, so please be careful when your dogs exit (and subsequently enter) the car. The trailhead starts straight out from the parking area. There are no trail maps or informational kiosk, but there is a green and yellow preserve sign.

State of Maine Wildlife Management Area and Nature Conservancy— Merrymeeting Bay (South Dresden)

Honorable Mention

There are two properties adjacent to each other here, creating a large area of land that is open and free for the public to explore. I would take precautions with off-leash dogs in the hunting season, since the map shows a large area that allows firearms, crossbows, and bow hunting. There are no marked trails or formal maps of the area, but the informational kiosk can tell you the property boundaries and give

you an idea of where *not* to go. Bring a compass or GPS unit. This is an adventure for those of you who consider yourselves trailblazers and explorers.

Directions: This preserve and wildlife management area is located between the Green Point Wildlife Management Area and Robert Tristram Coffin Flower Fields off Route 128. From Woolwich and U.S. Route 1 North, go left onto Route 127 North. Stay on Route 127 for 1.8 miles, then go left onto Route 128 North. Stay on Route 128 North for approximately 5.5 miles. Go left on Thwings Point Road (a dirt road). The parking area and property map kiosk are on your right, visible from the road (about 0.5 mile down this dirt road). If you continue past the map stand and parking area, you will come to a place where the road becomes a private drive and you are asked to turn around (via a sign). Please respect the privacy of those who own property adjacent to these public areas.

Summer Street Park (Lisbon Falls)

Honorable Mention

Dogs are permitted here, and there are a slew of trails to choose from, all with a different color scheme. The trails go underneath power lines and extend all the way to the Little Androscoggin River. All told, there are about 4 miles of trails. There is no map available other than the one drawn on the informational board, so take a good look at this sign as you leave your vehicle. Bringing a compass or GPS unit is a good

idea. There are actually a few different trailheads starting off Summer Street, and they join up at an open picnic area (with tables). The red trail is the longest. These are pretty dense woods, so bring your bug spray. Leave nothing but footprints behind.

Directions: If you are coming from the north, take Interstate 95 to Exit 80 and travel east on Route 196 through Lisbon. Summer Street will come in from your left after you have traveled through Lisbon and Lisbon Falls. The park will be on the right side of Summer Street 0.2 mile up the hill from Route 196. If you are coming from Topsham, Bath, or Brunswick, take Route 196 West out of Topsham. Stay on Route 196 approximately 5.6 miles from the intersection of Route 201 and Route 196 in Topsham. You will approach Lisbon, but Summer Street will come in from the right before you go into town. Turn right on Summer Street and head up the hill. The information kiosk is on your right. Park off the pavement as best you can. The shoulder can be soft. Let your dogs out of your vehicle with caution.

Sweetsir Lot (Yarmouth)

Honorable Mention

Slightly hard to find, but it's a decent out-and-back trail that goes down to the northern part of the Royal River. This is a single-track logging road or ATV track. There is no organized trail map or trail blazes on the trees, but

the trail is wide enough to follow without markers. The trailhead is a bit hard to locate. It starts from the parking pad; look to the left side of your vehicle and into the woods between the last house's driveway (on your left) and the parking pad. The path leads through thick woods, and the bugs are numerous in the summer months, so make sure you bring bug spray. You need to return the same way back to your vehicle. This is fairly flat terrain and in the late summer it is overgrown with weeds.

Directions: Take Interstate 295 either north or south to Exit 17 for Yarmouth/Freeport. Take U.S. Route 1 South for 0.3 mile to East Main Street. Go right on East Main Street and then turn immediately left on North Street. Stay on North Street for 1.6 miles. Go left on Concord Circle; this takes you into a housing development. After 0.2 mile you will come to a large circular roundabout—go to the right half-way around. Then take Old Field Road to the right at the apex of the roundabout; go to the very end (approximately 0.2 mile). There is a house with a single lane driveway on the left and a "parking pad" (elevated, paved, square parking area) at the end of the road. The trailhead is barely visible on the left side of the parking pad if you have your back to your vehicle.

Tedford Road Power Lines / ATV Trails (Topsham)

Overall Score	🐾🐾	Difficulty	🔥🔥
Average Time	45 mins.–2 hrs.	Parking	🦴🦴🦴
Average Distance	3.0 miles	Trail Markings	None

A vast network of off-road vehicle trails that run primarily under power lines. It is a good place to bring dogs, because no private properties are near the trails, so your pets have free rein. I have not met any ATVs here to date, but based on the wear and tear that can be seen on the trails, it is wise to keep an eye (and ear) out so you can call your dogs back to you if motorized vehicles suddenly appear. Wild turkeys seem to like it here, as well as deer, and hunting is allowed, so wear blaze orange in the fall or avoid this area in the hunting season. Dogs do like to chase wildlife, so be aware of this before you go. Although you will be following power lines, bringing a compass or GPS unit is not a bad idea.

Directions: Off U.S. Route 1, coming south from Bath take the Topsham/Route 196 Exit (the first exit for Topsham). Go north to the first lighted intersection (of Route 196 and Route 24). Go right here, and then take the immediate next left; this is Middlesex Road (Route 24 N). Alternately, if you are coming north on Interstate 295, take Exit 31 for Topsham/Route 196. Go south on Route 196 toward Brunswick. As you come down a long hill toward the U.S. Route 1 on-ramps, go left at the last lighted intersection, which is the intersection of Middlesex Road (a.k.a. Route 24) and Route 196. Then take the immediate next left; this is Route 24 N. After no more than a few hundred feet take the next road to the left; this is Tedford Road. After 0.5 mile on Tedford Road veer left into a dirt parking lot and keep driving straight. You will see the ATV tracks under the power lines. Park off the roadway or in the gravel lot.

Thorne Head Preserve (Bath)

Overall Score	🐾🐾🐾	Difficulty	🔥 🔥
Average Time	30 mins.–1 hr.	Parking	🦴🦴
Average Distance	0.5–1.5 miles	Trail Markings	★

A very busy dog-walking area. You are likely to meet people with pets here at any time of year. The trailhead starts right from the parking lot, past the metal gate or off to the left into the woods. There are free maps and information about the Lower Kennebec Regional Land Trust, which owns this property. The map is terribly inaccurate in terms of illustrating the actual trails, but it does show the overview of the land preserve so you can get your bearings. Most people walk up to the top of the overlook, where there is a stone table. It is 0.43 mile from the parking area to the stone table. However, there are many other trails to choose from, and you can even make a loop if you are so inclined. The trails to the right of Overlook Trail are not marked, but they are so well trodden it is easy to find your way. The trails to the left of Overlook Trail (Landfill Lane or Traverse Trail, for example) are marked with light blue trail blazes on the trees. A perimeter trail skirts the margins of the Kennebec River. This water has a severe current, so keep a close watch on your dogs if they go for a swim. Some of the traversing is a bit steep and requires good shoes. People do come here without dogs, so please respect those who might not want to be accosted by a wagging or slobbering four-legged pet. Please bring your own poop bags, and it is not a bad idea to have a leash with you.

Not all dogs are equally well socialized, so keep an eye on your pets when you see others ahead of you on the trail (or through the trees). The trails get extremely icy in the wintertime.

Directions: Take U.S. Route 1 North to Bath, exiting at High Street/Phippsburg, which is the second exit within the Bath town limits; go left (north) onto High Street. If you are coming from the north, exit U.S. Route 1 as you come over the bridge (over the Kennebec River from Woolwich to Bath) and go straight down the hill to the first light. Go right here; this is Washington Street. At the next light go left on Center Street and up the hill to High Street. On High Street go right—the Androscoggin County Court House and Sheriff's Office are on your left—kitty-corner to you. Go north on High Street (keeping straight at every intersection) until it ends (literally). This will be approximately 2 miles from the Center Street/High Street intersection. Thorne Head Preserve starts where High Street dead-ends. The parking area is packed dirt and gravel.

Topsham Fairgrounds (Topsham)

Honorable Mention

Large fairground area and some ball fields with lots of nooks and crannies to explore. There is a small sand track for horses, lots of small buildings intermingled with clusters of pine trees, tremendous amounts of things to smell, green grass to run on, and manure to roll in. (You have been warned! One of my dogs rolls in the horse manure every time we come here.) People in cars do use the road going through the fairgrounds as a shortcut, so be careful if you walk on the main thoroughfare. Several locals walk their dogs here off-leash, but the area is so large that you likely won't meet many others. Please bring your own poop bags and clean up after your pets. The fair is usually

held during the first week in August, so I would recommend staying clear of this area at that time of year. (If you want to go to the fair, your dogs can't come along.)

Directions: Off U.S. Route 1, coming south from Bath toward Brunswick, take the Topsham/Route 196 exit. Go north (veering right) on Route 196 approximately 1.2 miles (toward Topsham Mall and Interstate 295), and you will come to a lighted intersection. Go left on Governors Way; there is a large Red Cross building on your left. As you enter the fairgrounds, slow down and look for a place to park off the pavement. If you are coming north on Interstate 295, take Exit 31, Topsham/Route 196. Go south on Route 196 toward Brunswick. At the intersection of Route 196 and Governors Way (a traffic light), go right and follow it down about 0.1 mile to get to the fairgrounds.

Topsham Ravine/Highland Trails (Topsham)

Overall Score	🐾🐾🐾🐾	Difficulty	🔥 🔥 🔥
Average Time	1–1.5 hrs.	Parking	Off-street
Average Distance	1–2.5 miles	Trail Markings	★★★

A peculiar location but truly a wonderful set of trails in a cool, dark, damp, yet beautiful part of Topsham. Parking may prove to be a challenge, but there are some options that will afford you and your dogs access to these trails. Some of the trails are more challenging than others, but they all connect at one point, and they all run in a ravine or gully between a housing development (The Highlands) and Pleasant Street. Dogs are allowed here, and dogs that like water will undoubtedly get wet in one of the multiple water crossings. Some patrons choose to walk their dogs on a leash, so please respect them and control your off-leash dogs. Please bring your own poop bags so you can clean up after your pets. Currently there is no map, so even though the trails are well marked, keep your wits about you so you can get back to your vehicle using the correct returning trail.

Directions: This property is in a bit of a challenging location, but here are your access choices:

Off U.S. Route 1, coming south from Bath toward Brunswick, take the first Topsham exit, Topsham/Route 196. Go north on Route 196 approximately 1.2 miles (toward Topsham Mall and Interstate 295). Go left on Governors Way (second set of traffic lights), toward the Topsham Fairgrounds. Take the next immediate right into The Highlands housing development. This is designed to be a gated community (at the time of this writing the gates were left open), but you can take the dirt road on the right directly in front of the gate, which leads to the construction entrance. Travel about 120 feet on this dirt access road and park off to the left side of the roadway; the trailhead is directly across the lot, and you can see the white trail blazes and the sign "Highland Trails" on a tree. This trailhead is parallel to Route 196, which is very busy, so you may want to bring leashes for this portion of the trail.

Another option is to take the second Topsham exit, U.S. Route 1 South (from Bath to Brunswick). This exit takes you to Route 201 North. As you come off the exit ramp, set your odometer. You will be traveling over a bridge and past the Sea Dog Brewery (on the right). After 1.1 miles you will see a Volvo dealer, a Gibbs gas station, and the big brown Wright-Pierce building, all on the right side of the road. If you can park at any of these establishments (ask permission first), a trailhead can be located upon entering the woods behind the Gibbs gas station (slightly to the right of the Wright-Pierce parking area as you look at the woods).

A third option, if school is not in session, is to park at the Williams-Cone Elementary School and catch the trailhead that starts at the back of the school's property, past the playground. This school is on Perkins Street north of Route 24 or off Pleasant Street, east of Route 201 (heading north toward the intersection of Route 201 and Route 196) in Topsham. Park in the school's lot and walk to the back, left corner past the playground.

Twin Brook Recreation Area (Cumberland)

Overall Score	🐾🐾🐾	Difficulty	🔥
Average Time	1–2 hrs.	Parking	🦴🦴🦴
Average Distance	1–4 miles	Trail Markings	★★

This was once a 140-acre hayfield and is now a 240-acre recreation area. Well-marked trails run through the fields and into the woods. The trail surface is made of wood chips. Some of the trails are at times closed because of erosion, so please respect these signs if you see them and stay off those trails. There are picnic tables and toilet facilities. Lots of people come here to let their dogs run off-leash. This place is open all year.

According to the Town of Cumberland web site, dogs must be under the control of the person in charge of them at all times. All dogs must be leashed if in the areas of the playing fields when games or practices are in progress. During the non-winter months, dogs may be walked on all pasture areas and trails (except when the trails are in use for a running event), but may not be walked on the playing fields. During the winter months, dogs may be walked or sledded in any area except for the groomed ski trails. "The person in charge of a dog is responsible for cleaning up dog waste and will be strictly liable for any personal harm or damage caused by the dog," quoted from the town web site.

The parking area is gated and closes at sunset. There are several different places where you can park; most pet owners seem to drive all the way to the innermost gravel parking spot.

Directions: Take Exit 15 off Interstate 295 and look for signs for U.S. Route 1 South. Take U.S. Route 1 South, go about 0.9 (almost 1) mile, then go left up a hill and immediately right again, which will put you on Tuttle Road. Tuttle Road goes over U.S. Route 1. If you go under this bridge, you will have to turn around and go back. After getting onto Tuttle Road, go 1.6 miles, and Twin Brook Recreation Area is on your right. Enter the long, snaking drive and park anywhere in the parking lots. Bring your own poop bags and some fresh water for yourself and your dogs.

Webber-Kelly Preserve (Georgetown)

Overall Score	🐾 🐾	Difficulty	🔥 🔥
Average Time	1 hr.	Parking	🦴 🦴
Average Distance	1–3 miles	Trail Markings	★ ★

A fun and woodsy walk, but not great in the summer or fall due to mosquitoes and horse- or deerflies—bring repellent. The area was recently opened officially under the auspices of the Lower Kennebec Regional Land Trust (LKRLT). There is an official trail map, but it does not

list all the trails (which might mean that either the trails or the map is a work in progress). For example, the Quarry Trail, marked with a light blue sign, is not on the map and not marked with tree blazes, but you can follow it quite easily down to a stone quarry and get a decent view of Robinhood Cove (no water entry). There are a variety of other trails that are all marked with light blue paint (blazes) on the trees. The main trailhead starts up a small incline (away from the parking area), and at the top you can go left (Stonewall Trail) or right (down toward the Quarry trailhead). The trails are easy to moderate and take about 1 hour to complete if you utilize all the various out-and-backs. The woods are very dense, with some moist areas, so wear good shoes. A man-made bridge has been erected across the worst mud-area. There is wildlife in these woods, and your dogs may decide to take off on a scent or chase down a deer or two, so be alert. It is possible to walk down to a rock outcropping where a plaque has been mounted in memory of Webber-Kelly, who donated this property to the LKRLT. Leave nothing but footprints and pawprints behind when you depart.

Directions: This preserve is in Georgetown on the way to Reid State Park. Take U.S. Route 1 either north or south to Woolwich. In Woolwich follow the signs for Reid State Park and Georgetown by taking Route 127 South for 8 miles (nearly 8.1 miles). You will pass Georgetown

Pottery (on your right as you are traveling south), and the very next road on the right is Bay Point Road—you are turning right directly in front of the Georgetown Fire Station. Stay on Bay Point Road exactly 2 miles. The parking area for the preserve is on the left. The parking area is gravel. The trailhead is to your right if you park nose in. You will see the Webber-Kelly Preserve (green and white) sign. Bay Point Road is busy, especially in the summer, because there is a campground further down from this preserve, so don't let your dogs run out into the road.

Whitefield Salmon Preserve (Whitefield)

Overall Score	🐾🐾🐾	Difficulty		🔥 🔥
Average Time	55 mins.	Parking		🦴🦴🦴
Average Distance	1.5–2 miles	Trail Markings		★★★

This 56-acre preserve is owned and maintained by Sheepscot Valley Conservation Association (SVCA). There are two different trails, both of which run alongside the Sheepscot River. It is very pretty, and there are plenty of places to enter the river for a swim. Along the trail there are sights to behold, which are described in the free map (available at the parking area's kiosk). Dogs are allowed off-leash. The trails

do not seem to be utilized very much, because the white trail (Salmon Trail) was quite overgrown by late-summer. There are wood pieces and small man-made bridges to get you and your canines over the wet areas. According to the handout, there are over 4000 feet of prime Atlantic salmon rearing and spawning grounds here. This preserve is a bit

of a drive, but a lovely place to go for an adventure. Trails are well marked, and there are benches for humans to sit on. Please bring your own poop bags and clean up after your pets.

Directions: Take U.S. Route 1 North from Brunswick through Bath and over the bridge past Bath Iron Works to Woolwich. Reset your mile counter on your car as you come across the U.S. Route 1 Bridge into Woolwich. Continue north on U.S. Route 1 for 8.6 miles; you will now be in Wiscasset. In Wiscasset go left (north) on Route 218 N for a total of 16.9 miles; you will travel toward and through Alna past the Alna Fire Station. Veer right on Route 218 N in Whitefield and continue to North White-field. In North Whitefield go left on Route 126. After 1.1 miles on Route 126 go right on Vigue Road. Travel on Vigue Road for 1.7 (nearly 1.8) miles, then go right on Howe Road. After 0.9 mile on Howe Road the preserve parking area is on the right—you will cross a bridge over the Sheepscot River after 0.8 mile on Howe Road. Park here and pick up the trailhead to the right of the information kiosk.

Wilson's Cove Preserve (Harpswell)

Overall Score	🐾🐾	Difficulty	🔥
Average Time	15–25 mins.	Parking	🦴🦴
Average Distance	0.7 miles	Trail Markings	★★★

This is a very short walk down to Wilson's Cove in Middle Bay, but it is pretty and beautifully maintained. The terrain is fairly flat and in spots very muddy and wet. The trail snakes through a dense forest and sometimes even seems to loop back on itself. This is a small and narrow property squeezed in between private residences and posted property signs. The small informational sign at the trailhead

Welcome to
WILSON'S COVE TRAIL

A preserve of the

Harpswell Heritage Land Trust

Please:

Open dawn to dusk only.

Pedestrian use only. Stay on the trail.

No motor vehicles or bicycles. No overnight parking.

Carry in, carry out.

Take only pictures. Leave only footprints.

No open fires or camping.

Dogs must be on a leash.

No hunting or discharge of firearms.

This trail is on private property. Please respect the owner's and neighbors' privacy.

Thank you
Harpswell Heritage Land Trust
PO Box 359, Harpswell, ME 04079
207-721-1121 • info@hhltmaine.org

does say that dogs should be on a leash so they don't run onto private property. As you get down toward the bay, the trees seem less dense, and you can see the glittering water through them. You come out on an overhang high above the water's edge, so there is no water access at this property. You will simply turn around and go back out the same way you came. All in all, an easy and short little jaunt that by no means disappoints. Bring your own poop bags and clean up after your pet.

Directions: Take U.S. Route 1 or Interstate 295 to Brunswick (Exit 28). Go into Brunswick and take Maine Street toward Bowdoin College. Turn right onto Route 123 South. Stay on Route 123 S for a little over 7 miles. The small gravel parking area is on the right side of the road. Pull into the parking area off Route 123. Be careful when unloading your dogs, since you are so close to this busy road.

Winslow Park (Freeport)

Seasonable—Honorable Mention

Dogs are only permitted here after October 13th and before May 1, but local residents who go here in the off-season say that the area is spectacular, fun, diverse, and good for off-leash canines. This is a camping area and picnic park where you pay a fee to utilize the facilities. The view out across Broad Sound is beautiful. This park is at the very tip of Staples Point, so Staples Cove is on one side and Casco Bay/Broad Sound on the other. Lots of blue herons, white egrets, seagulls, and other salt-water wildlife can be seen here. People often come to let their dogs play together in the off-leash-permitted months. Bring your own poop bags and clean up after your pet. You are ultimately responsible for the safety of yourself, other patrons, their pets, and your pets. Keep in mind that off-leash socializing should be a fun event for your dogs, as an addition to regular exercise—not instead of a daily walk or routine exercise.

Directions: To get here from north of Freeport, take Exit 20 off Interstate 295. Off the ramp head toward downtown Freeport; at the first light go right onto U.S. Route 1 South. Take the very next left, Pine Street. Travel on Pine Street for 1.4 miles until it comes to a four-way stop; take a right here onto S. Freeport Road. Travel a little over a mile on S. Freeport Road, then go left on Staples Point Road. The park is at the very end of this road (about 1.4 miles). If you are coming from the south on Interstate 295, take Exit 17. Go north on U.S. Route 1 about 1 mile then go right on S. Freeport Road and drive 0.3 mile; go right again onto Staples Point Road. Winslow Park is 1.4 miles from here at the end of this road. Dogs usually meet for off-leash play past the second gate (out toward the point).

Index

Printed in the United States
208528BV00003B/190-525/P